10 STEPS TO *Almost* PERFECT PARENTING

Also by Mary Ellen Renna, MD

Medical Truths Revealed: Breaking the Misinformation Chain (2008)

Growing Up Healthy the Next Generation Way (2007)

10 STEPS TO *Almost* PERFECT PARENTING

Mary Ellen Renna, MD, FAAP

SelectBooks, Inc.
New York

This edition published by SelectBooks, Inc.
For information address SelectBooks, Inc., New York, New York.
First Edition

ISBN 978-1-59079-369-5

Library of Congress Cataloging-in-Publication Data

Names: Renna, Mary Ellen, author.
Title: 10 steps to almost perfect parenting / Mary Ellen Renna.
Other titles: Ten steps to almost perfect parenting
Description: First edition. | New York : SelectBooks, Inc., [2016]
Identifiers: LCCN 2015038224 | ISBN 9781590793695 (pbk. : alk. paper)
Subjects: LCSH: Parenting. | Child rearing.
Classification: LCC HQ755.8 .R457 2016 | DDC 649/.1–dc23 LC record
available at http://lccn.loc.gov/2015038224

Manufactured in the United States of America
10 9 8 7 6 5 4 3 2 1

For Sara, Spencer, and Jamie,
who make the world a better place for me.

Contents

Preface

We have all heard the saying that babies don't come with an instruction manual, but raising a baby into a healthy, productive, and happy adult is by far the hardest job on the planet. Any parent will attest to that statement. We only get one shot at being a parent. There are no do-overs, so it's important to try to get it right.

Parenting over the past few decades has become more of a partnership between parent and child where the child has the power to cajole, bargain, and at times even rule. As a pediatrician, the only expectations I have as to how a child should act in my office include their being respectful to others while in the waiting room and, of course, not hurting the doctor, assistant, or parent during the process of the exam. Nevertheless I am continually astounded at the behavior I see each day.

Adolescents, when asked, "So what brings you in today?" often don't even bother looking up from their cell phone to answer my question as I stand waiting for an answer. Or their answer might be, "How should I know why I am here?" in an extremely rude tone.

Children are told five or six times by their parents to "stop turning off the light" or "get off the iPad, honey, the doctor is here" before they even acknowledge that they were asked to do something, let alone follow the command given to them. Parents ask questions requesting permission from their young children, such as, "Do you want the doctor to give you the shot today?" Children refuse to cooperate when being examined or make demands like "I will do it, but *you have* to take me to the store and get me a video game."

Instead, I should hear "You are getting a shot today, sweetie" and "Honey, do as the doctor asked and open your mouth" in an authoritative but calm tone. This lets the child know that you are in charge and there is nothing to worry about; nothing horrible will happen during the doctor's visit.

There should be no lengthy discussion or bargaining in these types of situations. When asking a child to do something, there should be no need to say it more than once. If they don't listen the first time, a penalty must follow.

Parents must be the leaders and the decision makers. They should have expectations for their children's behavior, and hand out an appropriate consequence when expectations are not met. A punishment that is not upsetting to the child is an ineffective consequence for a bad behavior and will not discourage a repeat of the behavior. While this consequence should be one that is upsetting to the child, physical punishment should never be used. The most effective repercussions should be given out immediately—for example, taking the phone or game away from the child for a set amount of time. If this is not possible other options include canceling a playdate, or another fun activity that was scheduled for the day.

There is a lot of information to absorb about good parenting in these chapters, and it is understandable if it seems an almost impossible task to follow all the steps that will be presented.

But few things in life are impossible and nothing should stand in your way of attempting to do your job as a parent to the best of your abilities.

The first step discussed is to stop telling your children they are special people (except in so far as they are special to *you).*

Step 2 nudges parents to take a step back and stop micromanaging and controlling every aspect of their child's life.

Step 3, "Let Them Fail," may be the hardest of all. Holding back on your reflexive instincts to always catch your child before they fall or falter will allow them the experience of feeling disappointment. They will learn how to handle the feeling so that it's not new to them when they invariably experience it as an adult. Then they will not have a fear of failure, which will allow them to take chances!

Step 4 reinforces the rule that the parent is the boss; it's what every parent thinks they are already, but . . . not quite.

Step 5, "Become a Teacher," is instinctually obvious when read aloud but is not so easily enacted. There are so many issues to think about as a parent, but if we just take one event from each day and turn it into a valuable life lesson, we will become our children's greatest teacher.

Step 6 addresses how children learning to solve problems has become a dying art, and we had better do something quickly if we intend to have our kids live on their own. Problem solving is a fundamental technique that must be nourished to grow into a healthy skill.

Step 7, about being a good example to your children, is of the utmost importance, since your child will almost always do as you do, as opposed to doing as you say. Their eyes are always on their parents—listening and watching and learning even when you are not aware of this. If you are the driver who invariably rolls through stop signs and guns it at yellow lights, don't expect your child to drive differently. If you continually use foul language but tell your child not to curse, be prepared for them to curse. Remember to be the person you want your children to be!

Step 8, about not giving your children everything they want, is really easy to do, and will save your pocketbook while instilling values in your child.

Step 9 is a warning to parents who may not realize they are "parentifying" their children (asking a minor for adult advice and giving them responsibility for our well-being). Be their parent. We don't treat friends like they are our parents, so don't treat your children like they are your friend! It becomes too much for them to handle, and at the same time it takes away power from the parent. Don't be their friend! You are their parent, so learn to act like a one.

Step 10 is all about the danger of trying to make your children become something that's all your idea. It is a big reminder to not attempt to live your life through your child's life. Don't push your dream life onto your kid.

So here it is, the 10 Steps to almost perfect parenting. Having raised three children at home and guided thousands of parents at work, I realize the enormity of the task presented to modern parents: preparing the next generation for a happy productive life. Reading this book will help you identify areas that may need some work, while possibly also validating some areas that you have already nailed down. Each step that a parent can successfully carry out will bring him or her closer to raising a child who can and will do great things on a big or small scale.

Introduction

We cannot always build the future for our youth,
but we can build our youth for the future.

—Franklin D. Roosevelt
Address at University of Pennsylvania
(September 20, 1940)

For the past thirty years my life has been divided into two major aspects: being a parent and practicing pediatrics. While raising my own family and dealing with the crises and challenges that arise, I have also dealt head-on with the troubles and pandemonium that occurs in the lives of my patients. Drugs, death, defiance, divorce, bullying, financial and emotional instability—the list is endless. Generation after generation the list of issues to deal with rarely grows shorter, but rather larger and stranger. Technological advancements and social changes shift the course of the thinking and values of a new generation. With this shift comes the wave of advice on how parents should respond to these.

I have parented my three children, now adults, while at the same time observing my patients grow up and go on to become parents. Over this time I have been a witness to a disturbing trend between parent and children: children are controlling their parents instead of parents being in control of their children. I've seen those who overpraise their children, prioritizing friendship over parenting and giving them everything they ask for, while at the same time managing every aspect of their child's life and essentially harming the generation to come. We need to make a change and the sooner the better.

While children's minds are being formed, we must act quickly to mold how they learn and how they react to problems. No matter how old the child is, it's not too late to influence them, so get started now on getting it right. That means that *you* as a parent have to change. Whether we like it or not, whether for good or bad, this all starts with the parent's skill set. The purpose of this book is to teach parents how to change some of their behaviors and the way they react to their child. It might be hard to understand now, but having greater expectations for your children, giving them more responsibility, letting them fail occasionally, and being a real leader will provide them with growth, self-sufficiency, and true happiness.

Every new generation of parent marches through a learning curve. Habitually we take hold of the methods and ideas used by our parents, as they did with us. But with that inheritance comes the faults—faults that we naturally attempt to correct. Despite the fact that we live with, and alongside, other humans, when it comes to raising them, the concept of what's right and wrong seems to elude us. Before I wrote the first word of this book I already knew the title. I was honest with myself and I'm being honest with you—there is no such thing as a perfect parent and this book will not teach you how to be one. But gaining an understanding that what we were taught by our parents was not all wrong, and that our natural instincts aren't always right, we can begin to piece together an idea of where our minds need to be in order to be excellent parents.

We, to varying degrees, have a lot of privilege as parents in this day and age. This is a comfortable time for most. Throughout time, however, families were raised in the most perilous conditions. Colonists suffered through disease and dangerous sea travel. Pioneers crossed the Great Plains together;

they suffered and died of the horrors of living in earlier centuries. But in the face of those dangers, most of which thankfully disappeared in time with the advances in technology, children still grew to prosper and to raise the generations that followed. Hardships were met with tough skin and an uncompromising attitude—a mentality of survival and growth.

What did this do for the developing human? Was it the best environment to be raised in? Certainly not, since children were put into unacceptably dangerous situations as they were overworked, potentially undernourished, and exposed to dangerous diseases. The past should not always be seen as a model for how we approach the future. I am not advocating for a hardcore survivalist lifestyle. We should embrace our modern privilege. But there were some good qualities that children learned that were developed out of sheer necessity.

The children of yesteryear had demands placed on them that helped develop their self-esteem, their work ethic, and basic skills for problem solving and survival. These were helpful as the child grew into an adult who was prepared for life. Disappointment was not a novel experience, so when situations arose that involved failure this wasn't considered the end of the world to them. Hard work and other expectations of behavior placed on the child only nurtured the survival instincts that created a successful adult.

When cultures demand self-sufficiency early on, this evolves into the ability of children to tolerate a response of "no" to their requests and their learning to handle disappointment. Parents are empowering their children to have a good sense of self. This sense is akin to self-esteem and having a feeling of value. As the sense of one's self grows in the child, this brings on more confidence, which creates more independence and competence.

Parenting is not about being a partner with your child but being a leader and guide through their life. You make the rules only for the benefit of your child. You are there to teach them and steer them in the right direction, advise them, counsel them, and corral them when needed. When a parent is calmly in command and their sensible rules are being followed, it is natural for peace and tranquility to come next.

Today's society is at a crossroads of extremes about the philosophies of what makes good parenting, and it's time to get centered. The recommendations range from allowing young children to make important life decisions to suggestions that parents attend to almost every aspect of their child's daily activity. It seems children are also not being held accountable for their actions and all too often parental excuses are made for their less than stellar behavior.

A commercial that recently aired on television gave us a bleak glimpse into what parenthood has become in this millennia. Here is the scenario. A mom pulls up into the driveway in her mini-van having just returned from grocery shopping. The car full of groceries for the family must now be unloaded and brought into the house. Sitting on her front lawn are her two young sons. The eldest is playing a handheld game while the youngest is pretending to be a cowboy. The mother, with two large grocery bags in hand, calls out, "Boys can I get some help?" Her son playing with the handheld game makes a snarky remark without looking up, "I don't know, *can you*?" he replies, and continues to play his game without even looking at his mother. But once the promise of a junk food reward is announced he comes running over to help.

So where do we begin to explain the horror of this scenario? While a TV commercial is not a reality television show, the fact is that the bigger ideas being presented in this scene are so common that the media paints it as everyday life in order to sell us junk food. This type of behavior that's considered clever and humorous by parents is common and predictable. "They're just precocious kids" is the rallying cry behind this mentality, and it will quickly be our downfall as parents.

Most parents are quick to pass judgment on other parents. They judge the attitudes and actions of other children and how the parents react to them. When a situation arises that they are not a part of, like the one depicted in the commercial, they are able to clearly see that the child is being disrespectful and rude to his mother. However, when it is your own child behaving in this manner, the scenario then becomes at bit more invisible to the parental eye. It is a much more difficult task to see your own child acting in an egregious manner. All we see is our sweet little boy, whom we don't want to upset or make sad by expressing disapproval or pulling them away from their fun.

Parents can be blinded by their love for their child. A parent can convince himself that a little snarky remark was not really mean and unpleasant but just playful and really not meant to harm, so they allow it to pass. Or maybe it is just easier to do a chore without their help since the child adds another layer of difficulty and getting it done alone is quicker. Or maybe there is no expectation that a perfectly capable young man should help his mother with the packages and his having fun is more important than chipping in with the chores. Whatever the reasons, none of them are helping the child, and in fact *we are ensuring that the next generation will be entitled, angry, and disappointed.*

A first-time parent with a new baby is experiencing one of the most delightful of new emotions, the love of their baby, for the first time. It can be hard to be a fully rational adult while gazing into the eyes of the miracle baby that was just created. All your senses are awakened in a way you have never felt before, and your heart is ruling your life instead of your head. You do and say things you never thought possible, and now more than ever is the time to be a rational, intelligent adult as the responsibility of this new life is all yours. Reading this book will help guide you to channel the overwhelming emotions you are feeling into a more rational approach to make sure you mold your new son or daughter into a happy and healthy adult.

From the generation of families that suffered through the Great Depression to the first generation raised on television, we can learn from the past and blaze a trail into the future in order to become better parents. However, realizing that there is a problem is the first step. You can't cry freedom before you even notice the shackles around you. To accomplish that, you need to be honest with yourself, and take an objective look at your own actions, and that is where we will begin.

Step 1

Stop Telling Them They're So "Special"

If your ego starts out, "I am important, I am big, I am special," you're in for some disappointments when you look around at what we've discovered about the universe. No, you're not big. No, you're not. You're small in time and in space. And you have this frail vessel called the human body that's limited on Earth.

Neil deGrasse Tyson

From a 2014 interview with Bill Moyers during
the Moyers and Company airing of Carl Sagan's *Cosmos*

- *Overpraising hinders* children rather than building them up

- Remember that while they are *your special kids,* they are *not the world's special kids*

- Develop a successful mentality for your child by *praising their efforts* rather than intelligence or skill

When a new or expecting mother speaks about childbirth, one word springs to mind: miracle. Childbirth is a miracle and it's very easy to get swept up in the spiraling winds of euphoria and pleasure. You have given birth to new life, a young and loving child for you to raise and spend your days with. You gaze upon the new baby you have created and see a little beauty filled with massive potential who will do no wrong. The perfect little angel! You are right in your feelings and assumptions. After all, they have the sweetest smile, cutest face, the most endearing mannerisms, and the biggest heart.

Within them are endless roads of possibilities for them to travel down. Every time they look up at you with eyes fresh and new, that is what you see, and that is the way it is supposed to be for mere survival's sake. If we didn't absolutely adore our children, if we didn't worship the ground they walk on, it is likely that far fewer people would exist in the world. Who else besides the child's own parent is going to put up with the trials and tribulations a child puts their parents through? With this feeling comes a sacrifice that everyone knows about, but not everyone honestly and deeply considers. It's the punch line of every sitcom joke, but when it happens to you and your spouse, it's far from funny. It goes like this: No more weekend getaways on a whim or late nights with the guys. No more sleeping when we want to, or eating a meal when we want to, and sometimes it's hard to even use the bathroom without interruptions. All this is hardly given a thought in the beginning, as the new responsibilities of being a parent are happily taken on because you just created the *most amazing human on this planet!*

Your child is unique and the most wonderful person in **your** world and that is the way it should be. They need to know how loved they are; they need to feel that their parents are their strongest advocate and will move heaven and earth to protect them. They need to have that feeling of unconditional love from a parent. However, it is absolutely critical to make children understand they are not the most important person in *the entire world*.

Hearing the words "your kid is not special" usually brings an onslaught of emotions, none of which are pleasant. Most parents would challenge that claim and fight anyone who declared that their child was not a very special kid. Here comes the hard part. You need to understand that your child is especially important only to you and your loved ones. The trouble begins when a parent does not have the understanding that their child is not a remarkable human being to everyone and does not need to be treated as such. Once parents realize that their child is usually only special to them and a few others and begins to prepare their baby for the world—a world that will not view their progeny as anything but a typical human—only then will progress be made in molding the child into a successful, productive adult.

The planet has billions of people on it and most people fall into the average category, most likely including your kids. It's a hard nut for a parent to swallow. Of course there are many children who have exceptional talents in some areas, but this does not make them anymore important than a child who does not excel by societal standards. Even in the rare case of a child prodigy, it is important to keep them grounded.

Every parent sees their child as a wonderful gift, but the rest of the world does not have the same view. This goes against what most parents see as a reality. How can it be that the little human you created is *not* special, amazing, wonderful, a sight to behold? It just does not seem possible. Even more baffling is the fact that parents were told they needed to make their child feel important, and it was imperative to heap on the praise. Build up their confidence and bolster their ego to make that special child feel exactly that—unique and astonishing.

With a serious and critical look at ourselves, how many humans really fall into the category of being "special"? Mother Teresa and Martin Luther King Jr. (of course we could make the case for a few more) are maybe two humans out of the billions who have walked this earth in the past hundred years who really do fall under the realm of being truly extraordinary. The rest of us who have traversed the earth fall under the very boring realm of being your average, ordinary human being. Some will have more talent, more intelligence, more physical strength, or even a rare skill, but if you truly love your child, you will raise them without having them think they are above anyone else.

In the now famous high school commencement speech by David McCullough Jr., he reminds us, "Even if you're one in a million, on a planet of 6.8 billion that means there are nearly 7,000 people just like you." Being one of seven thousand people does not make a person special. It is sobering to think in those terms, but parents need to start to think along those lines if they are truly interested in what is best for their children.

So how and why do we need to do that? Parents in Generation X, the generation born between 1956 and 1980 following the baby boomers, were taught that it is imperative to a child's feeling of self-worth that they are praised frequently. If there is a failure at building up their self-esteem, if we don't praise them enough, we will be crippling their future self. The threat looms that they won't be able to grow into a wonderful, successful, confidant, and happy adult. So we must garnish them with love, admiration, and accolades to our fullest capabilities. We must nurture them by telling them how wonderful they are and how important they are. Their self-esteem is built up by praising them for every task they accomplish.

Parents are sent into a fit of jumping up and down when their eighteen-month-old builds a block tower, thinking their child will be the next great architect. "How amazing is that block tower?" they exclaim to their little prodigy. The parent of a precocious four-year-old hangs on every word declaring, "Isn't she the most loquacious talker?" The parents of a sixth-grade honor student drive around with a sticker proclaiming to the whole world "My kid is an honor student." The adolescent who plays on the winning baseball team in school is constantly told "You're an amazing athlete!"

Parents are told that making their child feel important will help them build up the confidence they need for life. So it's a natural response when parents do everything in their power to make their child feel that essential emotion. A common situation is when a parent allows a child to continually interrupt a conversation between two adults. The parent will stop the conversation with the adult to answer their child's inquiring words, not realizing how rude it is to the other adult. This is done in an attempt to make sure the child feels he is on equal ground.

He must never feel that he is not important enough to have his question answered as soon as it comes into his head, no matter what the parent is doing—talking on the phone or conversing with another adult.

Add into the mix the fact that parents are terrified of their kids just being average. Who wants average? If we build them up and heap on the praise we will make them exceptional. And telling a child how amazing and smart they are seems like the way to go.

Here comes the boom. It has been shown that this is not the right way to build true self-respect and confidence, and parents have been guided in the wrong direction for the past few generations. The last decade or so has been rife with studies designed to look at how attempts to build self-esteem by heaping praise on kids is affecting them, and the results are not what we expected. It appears to be contrary to what we've been taught. Continually giving your child praise and making them feel as if they are the chosen ones gives them an undue sense of self-importance. They have a more difficult time connecting with others. The whole cascade of effects then leads to insecurity and fearfulness.

Making your child feel as though the sun revolves around them, since they are the closest being to perfection this earth has seen, leads to feelings of arrogance. Constantly heaping on praise for achieving normal childhood developmental milestones is not helpful to them. Yes, being loving and supportive and using words like "I love you forever" is extremely necessary and needed on a regular basis. But it is okay to tell your four-year-old to wait until you are done talking with an adult before you address his very important query of "I want a lollipop now Ma, can I have it?"

The notion of not answering your child the minute he wants something, despite the fact that he is being taught to be rude by interrupting a conversation, goes against the parental grain. What is happening now is that we are raising children who are developing an overinflated sense of themselves and who are becoming downright entitled.

The feeling of self-importance a child may have comes through in small ways and big ways. Needing to be first in line "since I am so very important" or feeling that "I deserve the biggest cupcake" at a party. They will take on the "mine is better" attitude all the time since that's what they were told. Their sandcastle is always better, they can run the fastest and kick the hardest. "I am the best letter writer since I am so smart. My mom told me." No wonder they become little narcissists. When this cycle continues it is obvious why a child might have difficulty connecting with peers. Their growing sense of grandiosity leaves little that is desirable. The "special child" is not the likable child and other children will naturally shy away from them.

When a five-year-old entering kindergarten has spent the last five years of his life hearing that he was "so intelligent" and the "most amazing picture maker" and "a wonderful soccer player," imagine how he is going to feel when he realizes everyone else is pretty much like him. He was told he was smart and good at things, so he must be, but deep down inside, somewhere in the recesses of his brain, he is aware that he really is not so different from the other kids.

These conflicting realities breed insecurity, fear, and shame. This child will avoid a challenge for fear of failure. He has to be the best because his mom and dad always told him he was, and this means he has to be able to win all the time. But this is not possible in all situations. So the astute little kid will choose only challenges that are a guaranteed success to ensure that the "I am the best" reality can continue. He will avoid anything that could be an obstacle and lose out on many chances to have even greater success.

The fear of failing can become overwhelming for a five-year–old, essentially paralyzing him. If he does not do well, he will be forced to face the humiliation of not having lived up to being superior to his competitors. The cycle of avoidance will continue, and he will make excuses for any activity or challenge that will not be met with high achievement. What a burden placed on this little kindergartner! He has been set off on the wrong foot and it's up to the parents to reverse this trend.

More and more research is telling us that this culture of constant praise during a child's upbringing must come to an end or be retooled as to how praise is doled out. Psychologists have delved into how we need to do this with research that has some interesting and eye-opening results.

Carol S. Dweck, a psychologist and researcher, coined the terms "fixed mind-set" and "growth mind-set." In her research she has identified these two different patterns of children. Those who are of a "fixed mind-set" feel intelligence is a static entity and cannot be changed—it's a God-given gift that once appropriated by a person stays for good without change. These "fixed mind-set" individuals care more about how people perceive them and less about learning. It's important for them to be known as smart.

Because they are concerned with the perception of who they are, namely that they are smart, they avoid challenges that may not be successful so they don't look stupid. They only want a challenge that reinforces their intelligence. If they are truly smart, doing well does not require effort, so they don't need to study or work at it. A challenge that comes along that requires work will be instinctually deflected to protect what they hold to be true: intelligent people don't need to work to learn. Since their perception of intelligence does not include having to work for a good outcome, they will avoid challenges that don't come easily.

A child with a fixed mind-set will look something like Barry, a tenth grade student who is getting all A's. Up until this point Barry has had a pretty good time in school academically. He brags about never having to pick up a book and still gets amazing grades. His teachers all agree that he is a good student and a bright young man. His high school counselor recommends that he be moved to all honors classes. Barry is happy that his counselor sees how smart he is, but he is also worried about not doing well. He decides to take only one honors class in science since he was always told what a whiz kid he was in science. The new class begins and Barry is no longer able to get away with not doing any work. It is much harder than he anticipated, and he refuses to stay in the class. He drops it immediately without even taking the first test in the class.

Barry's "fixed mind-set" of being smart scared him away from the challenge of the advanced class. He would have been too embarrassed if he didn't do well, so he would rather drop the class than rise to the challenge of learning.

The "growth mind-set" coined by Dr. Dweck has a different view from the fixed mind-set. People with a "growth mind-set" view intelligence as a fluxing state. They believe, correctly, that intelligence and learning can improve with effort. They care less about whether they are seen as smart and more about the actual learning and the effort put forth. They are less fearful of a challenge and more apt to take on a difficult project.

What does a child with a growth mind-set look like? Let's go back to Barry, our tenth grade A student. When Barry's guidance counselor asks him to move into all advanced classes, instead of fearing that he may not do as well with a more difficult curriculum, he agrees to move to the full honors classes. With his growth mind-set he is not overwhelmed with worry that he may not always get A's and therefore no longer be seen as smart. His growth mind-set sees this as an opportunity to improve his learning and his skills. He takes on the challenge with gusto, hoping to work out his brain muscle to greater heights.

The end result is that the Barry in this scenario would take on the challenge and fare much better than the Barry who dropped out of the honors science class. The growth-minded Barry would have a better high school transcript, even if all his grades fell a little, than the fixed-minded Barry who took an honors class and dropped it. When colleges look over Barry's transcript the failure to complete the honors class will be more egregious than slightly lower grades in the honors classes.

By having an understanding of these different mind-sets we can explain what happens to the child whose parents overpraise them. Kids who are praised for their *intelligence* tend to develop a fixed mind-set whereas kids who are praised for the *effort* they put forth tend to develop the growth mind-set.

So what does this mean for your child in the real world? While a parent or teacher is throwing on the accolades about his or her intelligence, a child is learning they will be perceived and recognized only for their intelligence. While they may initially feel good about being seen as a well-performing smart kid, the research shows this situation is short-lived. The kids who are praised for intelligence get into the fixed mind-set and think intelligence and intellectual achievement can't change. When they are faced with a problem in school that requires more effort, and they don't rise to the occasion by working harder, they do less well. They then lose their confidence and are more likely to give up. The idea that praise boosts confidence was shown to have the opposite effect. Kids withdrew from even simple tasks that they did well on prior to being challenged. Their shaken confidence pulls them into a downward spiral. Praising them had the completely opposite effect; rather than building up confidence in their skills, it resulted in their being shaken to the core.

But the children who are praised for their effort instead of their intellectual capacities are more likely to move into a growth mind-set. This mind-set spurs on the desire to learn, since their positive reinforcement has been on the learning process rather than their innate ability or having a successful outcome. These kids are more likely to willingly face a challenge because they are less concerned with being perceived as smart and more interested in the work involved in meeting the challenge. They essentially are more likely to tackle a problem than run from it.

What does the reality of this look like? How can we take these principles and apply them to work? *If a parent starts to take small steps, they will begin to realize that making these small changes is not difficult and can have a huge effect.*

Let's look at some examples for different age groups. Jamie is a three-year-old who brings home a drawing of her family from school. The picture is a rather precocious one, as she has drawn her mother in great detail with arms, legs, eyes, and a nose. Jamie also drew her mom as the biggest person. Her dad is next to her mom in an outline form showing only his legs, and next to Dad are her siblings in progressively smaller and smaller sizes and less detail. Her mom marvels at the thought that went into this picture as it truly is worth a thousand words. Jamie's mom is the biggest emotional piece in her life, and this little girl knew enough to draw her in the biggest size with the most detail. How incredible! Jamie's mom is swelling with pride as she exclaims, "Oh my gosh, Jamie this is the most amazing picture I have ever seen! You are so wonderful and talented."

It is hard to criticize a mom for that reaction; after all, it seems that we are all programmed to be self-centered and see what we want to see, and we want to put a smile on our kid's face anytime we can. However, she is setting Jamie up to have a fixed mind-set. Her mom's short-sightedness caused her to make an over-exaggerated claim to make her child feel special, and it's probably one of many "you're amazing" praises.

Instead of using a generic overall praise, it is more helpful to use words that praise her for the *process* of the work she brought home. "Jamie, *you worked so hard* while drawing this picture." Or maybe, "I love how you *thought* about the colors to use in the drawing, and were able to show Mommy in so much detail." These words are geared more toward the work that was put into drawing the picture rather than "You're so talented and wonderful." The reinforcement is for variables that should be repeated, e.g., working hard on a project or thinking about the end result of the picture by picking out the colored pencils. Praising her for the work and effort she put in now reinforces Jamie to move into a growth mind-set, which is more likely to bring her success as she grows up.

The fifth grader who is learning how to play the piano can be praised with "I love hearing you play; you are a little Mozart" fostering the fixed mind-set. Or you can say, "You practiced so hard today; that's wonderful," which is fostering the growth mind-set.

The adolescent who made a sculpture in art class will most likely be told, "You are a Michelangelo in the making," rather than being praised for the time he spent after school to finish the project.

When the outcome is not one that a student would want, for example receiving a C-minus on an essay that took hours to write, the parent should still focus on giving a thumbs-up to encourage the time and work that was put into the essay. After all, everything in life takes effort, but not everything will be success-ful. If we garnish every accomplishment, big or small, with heaps of gushing "Golly, you are the greatest!" we are forgoing *how* the accomplishment was achieved, which is the most important part to reinforce.

In the real world, it may not be so easy to remember to praise the process, as parents are too invested in making sure their chil-dren's ego gets stroked on a daily basis. It may be a hard habit to break. The fear that parents have of not reassuring their kids on a constant basis will be hard to quell. Some parents may decide that they know best and let their anxious emotions rule. The fear is too overwhelming that they might possibly hinder the solid development of their kid's ego.

Parents have been so ingrained to bolster their children with praise that it becomes a hard idea and habit to change, but just look around to see that something is amiss. Living proof is around us. The boomerang kids graduate from college but can't navigate into adulthood without coming back for a while. Society has seen an increase in arrogant, self-entitled adults because their parents heaped on the praise. Stand in line at a store and listen to how people talk to the folks waiting on them. The self-important, I-am-special, arrogant generation is all around. We don't need any more proof that parents are doing something wrong.

A fine line needs to be walked as we nurture our children. Giving words of encouragement are still in order as you stand by the soccer field and watch your daughter kick in the winning goal. It is still okay to say, "That was great! I am proud of you," but add in the ever so important "I am proud of how much you practiced" to make it a praise that encourages the growth mindset. If a parent can be a little more aware of how they are phrasing words to their children, it will make a huge difference. The grade-school child who breezes through his homework and does well on every test in school should not be told, "What a little genius you are," but instead be praised on getting his homework done each night or be told, "How wonderful it is that you pay attention and work hard in class."

The toddler who insists that he wants to show everyone how he can tie his shoes can be reminded, "Not everyone wants to see you tie your shoes, but I am *very happy you are working so hard and practicing.*"

A reminder is to rephrase your words and the praise you want to give. How you express your excitement about your child's accomplishment can help the process of reinforcing the actions you want your child to repeat, such as working hard at doing homework.

This de-centering of the child from being at the very center of the universe is a solid move in the right direction. It will help them have a better shot at becoming successful adults who are not arrogant, entitled, fearful narcissists.

Step 2

Stop Micromanaging

It's not what you do for your children, but what you have taught them to do for themselves that will make them successful human beings.

Ann Landers

From *Ann Landers Says Truth Is Stranger* by Ann Landers

- The hovering helicopter parents breed anxiety in their children

- Micromanaging your child's life can cause a failure to launch

- Over-involved parents encourage **learned helplessness**

The definition of micromanaging is controlling every part of an activity, large or small. In businesses when bosses micromanage they become too involved in every aspect of running the business and don't delegate well. This prevents the employee from learning the skills that are needed to be a productive part of the company. Corporations that are run by bosses who micromanage ensure the failure rather than the success of the company.

In the family dynamic, the parent who is the micromanager, or the "helicopter parent," casts a dark shadow of control over every nuance in the life of their child. They continually hover around their child, making sure to attend to every little detail, from what they do at the playground and their choices for meals to their sports activities, school activities, and selection of friends. The micromanaging parent is the *too-involved* parent! While the parent is busy orchestrating every detail of their kid's life to ensure her success, a major failure is likely to occur as a direct result of the micromanaging parent who never lets a child blossom into an adult able to manage their own problems or earn a living and fend for themselves.

Parental over-involvement through the years is now familiar to college administrators who are seeing more and more students struggling with anxiety and adjusting to independence and their new relationships. This is a direct result of the micromanaging parent! Parents are sending children off to college who are emotionally crippled because they have never learned how to manage their life. How can they hope to be successful?

Being an involved parent is very helpful to the growing child. It can help with their confidence and breeds a good sense of family, self, and support that will help a child grow into the productive adult that parents are hoping for. However, the overly intrusive parent creates a child that runs the risk of not evolving a strong sense of self. The belief that they "can do it" may never develop. Instead they are being taught ways that encourage helplessness. This in turn can lead to anxiety—and the anxiety this generation of children is experiencing seems to be at an all-time high.

Identifying anxious children is important because if anxiety disorders are left untreated they run a higher risk of substance abuse, school failure, and depression. Preventing the development of anxiety is obviously the better way to go. Children who have a genetic tendency toward problems with anxiety have the worst in them brought out by over-involved parents, but if their parents take a less involved approach to relationships with their children the tendency to be anxious can be lessened. In looking deeper into the cause of the anxiety epidemic, there is more than one reason behind this new trend, but the micromanagement of children by parents is certainly a main contributor.

Parents that attempt to manage many aspects of their child's life are at risk of essentially paralyzing their child. The child misses out on the many opportunities to learn how to react to a situation and manage their life because their parent "took care of it." Let your child do things without your help; it will go very far toward helping them in the long run.

Examining the past may reveal some reasons why a person becomes a micromanaging parent. The most apparent reason comes from the innate personality of the parent. An especially anxious mom or dad may be too afraid to let their child venture into a project without the guiding hands of their experience and protection. Another innate characteristic seen in the over-involved parent is the need to control every aspect of life. (Some controlling personality types stem from being overly anxious while others stem from lacking self-esteem.) Then there are parents who see themselves in their offspring and desire to relive their own childhood to fulfill a dream they were unable to realize. They will stop at nothing to ensure their child succeeds at everything so they can either live or relive a dream through their child.

There is also a subset of controlling parents who were raised in a household that was the complete opposite of over-involved parenting. They were raised with completely uninvolved parents who never attended baseball games or commented with pride when they received a trophy for the spelling bee. These new parents made a vow that they would always be a participant in their children's lives but overstepped their role and became too involved.

Whatever the reason, it is important to be able to identify a micromanaging parent, and it is helpful to recognize if you have any of these characteristics. Understanding why a person acts in a certain way goes miles toward helping the behavior change. If you can identify these traits or a past history early on, it will help you be more aware of the tendency toward over-parenting and perhaps sidestep the problem all together.

There are signs a parent needs to be on the lookout for that will enlighten them. For some the evidence even extends as far back as the child's infancy—yes, infancy! Pediatricians can see the evolution of the over-involved parent from the first few baby visits. The parent who is obsessed over every detail in their baby's life is starting to become a micromanager.

Of course parents must be aware of their baby's physical wants and needs and they must always know if something is wrong or out of the ordinary, but it is not necessary to be on top of every gaseous emittance, gurgle, or noise a baby makes. The parent who stands over the crib and watches the baby breath out of sheer terror that something may go wrong is well on the path to becoming an overbearing parent. Common sense should always reign, and for the most part new parents of a healthy baby should spend more time enjoying their infant and less time worrying about what might go wrong.

As the baby grows into a toddler, parents may start to track every morsel of food their child puts into his or her mouth. The parents have then become unduly concerned with the notion that their healthy, thriving child is not getting enough nutrition. From the yogurt they ate in the morning to the chicken nugget they took a bite of at the end of the day, parents spend their days chasing the child to attempt to get more food inside their bellies. (By the way, this is a battle that should never even get started, as the child will always win if forced to eat.) The parents' constant control of each food item ingested along with their worry that it was not enough results in a nightmare of micromanagement.

There is no need to keep track and obsess over what your toddler is eating; a parent merely needs to know that they are supplying only healthy food choices for their child. That does not mean making two or three different meals for your child because he refused to eat the healthy meal you made for dinner. If you like to do so, it is fine to engage your child in the food decision before the meal is made by giving them two choices. For example, you might ask, "Would you like to have chicken and string beans or salmon and broccoli for dinner tonight?" This may well be met with "Yuck I don't want that," in which case the parent will make the decision.

Once everyone is sitting and eating, and there are healthy food items on the toddler's plate, he will then decide which to eat. As long as you supply the meals, the toddler will eat when he is hungry enough. There's no need to worry that your child will go to bed hungry as long as food is available—a luxury that not all children have. No child will starve given the opportunity to eat. The complete and utter terror that parents experience over the possibility that their child might be hungry is useless. It only serves to ignite the flame of over-parenting at the food level. They start to cook up multiple different meals, insisting that something must be eaten even if the toddler is not hungry. This in turn may bring on disordered eating behaviors as the child grows.

The micromanaging parent will take a five-year-old to the playground, and instead of letting him wrangle with the play equipment and interact with the other children, the parent will be in the mix with the child. The literal and figurative shadow of the parent is cast on the child, as he never lets him out of arms reach. He is coaching him to go on the slide, then to the jungle gym, then to the swing set. He is continually orchestrating the playtime! By not allowing the young child to formulate their own free time, the parent starts to inadvertently dampen the child's sense of worth and self-esteem. How can a young child be confident if a parent does not allow them to venture into a play area and express their own desires in the play arena?

Now bring into the mix a child who is more aggressive than your child. The new child insists on going up the slide first, even though it's not his turn. The over-involved parent immediately scolds the boy for not waiting his turn rather than allowing his son to deal with the situation. As long as no bodily harm is imminent, the father should let his child work it out for himself. Allowing the child to fend for himself helps to build up his prefrontal cortex, the thinking part of the brain. Building up this part of the brain may help to stave off anxiety, and helping to stave off anxiety is an investment in your child's future. Think of it as building up the "brain muscle." Whenever you get the urge to intervene when it's not needed, remind yourself that you are literally building up your child's brain if you let him work out the issue alone. Let his abilities thrive, even if it goes against your natural instincts.

As the child gets older and moves into grade school, more evidence of the micromanaging parent comes out. If you are the parent and you have a third grader at home, it is safe to assume that you have already finished the third grade. This means that you don't need to do it again. So when your child comes home from school it is not your job to go over all his papers and read his homework assignment. It is not your job to sit with him and do each page of his homework with him. The desire of a parent of a grade-schooler is that he will excel in academics and do well in school. This is a craving of most loving parents, but how we go about letting it happen is what separates the parental styles into good and not so good.

The parent who takes out the homework, sits with the child until each page is complete, and intercedes with each task is not helping the child. It does not matter what the parental motivation is at this point, whether it's guided by anxiety that your child won't pass math or get into college, or from another anxiety.

What matters is that you did not allow your child to do the work—not just the actual homework, but the mental organization and preparation for getting it done by having the right books, reminding themselves that homework is due, and then going through the homework and finishing the tasks required.

The child can always turn to the parent if they are stuck or need help, but this does not give the green light for the parent to then take over the task until its completion. This means merely answering the question posed by the child and then letting him finish. Allowing the child to do his own work builds up the skills he needs as he gets older. He will not learn how to be successful if he does not learn how to do simple tasks like learning how to study or do his schoolwork. He must navigate through life without Mom or Dad by his side when he is a grown man at work, but he won't learn the skills if his parents do the work for him when he is young.

A parent who attends his daughter's soccer game should be there to cheer his daughter on, not keep track of how much time she played in the game or argue whether the foul was a fair call. The parent that starts to scream and yell at the coach or even other kids on the team is the over-involved parent.

At the lacrosse game are you standing on the sidelines prompting your son to move toward the goal or pass the ball? Or maybe after the game you tell him that he should have run to the goal in the second quarter or passed more often? Some parents see this type of behavior as merely giving out good advice and coaching the child to be a better lacrosse player, but did your child ask your opinion? Was he overly enthusiastic that you were trying to tell him how to play the game?

Take a step back and figure out why this behavior is occurring. The answer might be that you just want the best for your child and you want him to be happy. The natural follow-through is that if he plays lacrosse well he is sure to be happy. The other answer may be that you were a good lacrosse player in school and know your child could play better since he is your son. Whatever the reason, the result is that you are being a helicopter parent.

Trying to direct your child on the sidelines may only cause him disappointment, as he knows you're dissatisfied with his abilities. Even if you give the old high five and say, "Great game, son," the yelling and directing the game just tells him that he is not good enough or smart enough to play the game without your sideline direction. Just let him play the game and cheer him on. It's not your lacrosse game, it's his.

Parents that feel the need to participate in every aspect of their adolescent child's medical checkup appointment are clearly too involved. The mom who sits in on the checkup of her seventeen-year-old son and is chiming in on how he is feeling and answering the questions for him is an intrusive parent. These parents need to command complete control and don't feel confident that there child can properly convey all the issues that are important. This is over-parenting all the way.

The parent is so worried that their child will not have the ability to communicate medical issues to the doctor, even though he is a completely capable young man, that they will speak for him. This essentially is cutting your adolescent down and letting him know that you don't trust his ability to handle his own health issues.

The parent that calls up the high school teacher arguing that their child deserved a better grade each time a B or C was given is clearly too involved. It is the extremely rare occasion that a parent really needs to speak to a high school teacher, but unfortunately more and more parents are getting involved in micromanaging their high school child's grades for fear they won't get into a good college.

The children of these parents are missing out on some important life skills. If indeed they did deserve a better grade, they are the ones who should be doing the advocating. Your high school child is an adolescent who can use language to get his needs across. He is not a three-year-old going to nursery school for the first time. If he feels he deserves a better grade, let him speak to the teacher and fight for the grade. The parent that steps in to talk with a high school teacher for a better grade is disempowering their child. The reasons behind the action make sense if you feel your child was graded unjustly, but the action of attempting to speak to a teacher for your high school student is not justified.

Learning how to speak up and fend for themselves is an invaluable skill in life and needs to be encouraged. The over-involved parent must see that they are muffling the voice of their child. Instead it needs to be coaxed out of them so when the real world comes knocking on their door, they can handle it with ease. Unfortunately, the micromanaging parent stunts the development of the adolescent to become a self-advocate and subsequently inhibits the independence of their adolescent.

As college time approaches, the micromanaging parent does the legwork for the adolescent—from picking out the colleges, to filling out the applications, to even writing the college essay for the kids. The desire that each parent has to ensure their child gets into the best college supersedes their understanding of how over-parenting affects the long-term well-being of the adolescent. While the parent is busy organizing, orchestrating, and preparing for their child's entrance into college, they are watering the seeds of helplessness that have been sown in their child over time.

The parent is accomplishing nothing and is instead hurting their child. No matter how many times parents try to convince themselves that their kid needed help and could not have done it alone, there is no excuse for a parent who does the legwork for their kid. It must be the adolescent's responsibility to do most of the work to request information and applications, fill out the college applications, and write their essay.

While it is clear that the adolescent should not have carte blanche over which colleges to apply to (unless of course they are footing the bill), they should be the one doing the research and meeting with college advisors. By sitting down and filling out college applications with their older adolescent, a parent is silently telling their child that even though they are about to embark on a great journey, they still do not trust that what needs to get done will get done if left up to their child.

As a result of this treatment, the adolescent will struggle with emotional adjustment issues. It is understandable that the adolescent, who is in college, has a lower threshold for stress since the parent who took care of all the problems in the past is not around to help with the many issues that have now arisen in college. The college student must be responsible for getting out of bed on time to get to their 8:00 a.m. class because Mom is no longer around to pull him out of bed. He is the only one responsible for knowing when a paper is due now that the parent who perpetually stayed on top of their child's test schedule in high school is not there to keep track.

Daily tasks like making a bed, washing clothes, and getting food require planning and time management. These skills should be taught as a child grows. The micromanaged child is not given the proper guidance to become proficient in daily life tasks. The micromanaging parents have been more adept at clipping the wings of the young adult than letting them learn to fly on their own. As a result, we are seeing more and more of the college kids coming from a helicopter household fall short in their overall coping skills.

One theory about the rise in alcohol abuse on college campuses points to the helicopter parent at its root. This may help to explain the enormous increase in drinking among college kids. These young adults who have not fully developed their coping skills can turn to alcohol or other gateway drugs as a means to handle the new pressures. The young adult is faced with a college curriculum in a new social setting away from the comforts of home and is expected to not only survive, but hopefully to thrive. Alcohol is easy to acquire and gives the young college student a means to escape the pressures. Binge drinking is especially common on campuses as it allows the sheltered adolescent to say, "Look at me, I can make my own decision," while imbibing dangerous amounts of alcohol, ironically making them feel more in control. This perilous trend needs to be reversed.

If you are an over-involved parent, the first step is recognizing that you do too much for your child. Start by slowly backing off and giving more independence to your child. Use the small arena to start backing off and gradually add on bigger tasks. For example, stop tying your six-years-old's shoes every day simply because it's easier and quicker when you do it. Take the time and let this one little task be managed by your child. Next, perhaps allow him to pick out his outfit for the school day—no arguing about what he should wear as long as it fits the school dress code. Don't intervene if your child does not want to wear the shoes his grandpa got for him and instead wants to wear his well-worn sneakers. This should not be a battle.

The micromanaging parent may feel defeated at the loss of control, but this will soon be replaced with contentment when your child is getting dressed and ready for school without your help. The battle will have ended and with the over-parenting lessened, leaving a happier child with a better idea of how to do a daily task on his own. Those are big steps in the right direction, with the most important being the development of the child's decision-making skills and sense of independence.

Other ways to micromanage less is to let your child come to you for help with homework instead of you pulling out the books and laying them on the table to start the homework session. When your child asks you for help, do more listening and less talking. Resist the urge to take over the assignment with him. Answer his question and let him finish. Don't hover and wait for the next problem. If he does not finish all the work that was assigned, he is the one who will have to answer to the teacher.

A parent's instinct is to worry that if the child is not prompted to do the schoolwork, he will not only fail to finish the work, but may not even be capable of knowing what assignments have to be done in the first place. Children are very adept at sensing this lack of trust and will use it to their full advantage to get all the help they can from the nervous parent. When a child asks for help, offer the guidance they asked for and step away. If they are asking you to do too much, recognize that it's not your job and they will never learn if you do it for them. It is far better to leave your child alone to organize and complete his grade-school work, as this will serve to develop his skill sets and build his "brain muscle."

It's never too late to start to pull back and let kids take more responsibility. Asking the micromanaging parent to do less worrying about their child is akin to asking them to cut off an arm. Parents who are programmed to be anxious will have a harder time stepping back to let their child fend for themselves at first, but it is important to remember that the child who is never taught how to walk will never know how wonderful it is to run. Parents that attempt to manage many aspects of their child's life are essentially paralyzing their child. The child misses out on the many opportunities that can help them learn how to react to a situation and manage their life because their parent "took care of it." Let your child do things without your help; it will go very far toward helping them to be successful and happy in the long run.

Step 3

Let Them Fail

It is impossible to live without failing at something, unless you live so cautiously that you might as well not have lived at all, in which case you have failed by default.

J. K. Rowling

Harvard Commencement Speech, 2008

- Use failures as a means to build your child's brain connections

- Learning how to fail is an essential life skill

- The seeds of wanting to achieve success are planted in childhood

The definition of failure is to not succeed, to have been unable to perform or complete something that was due. It may seem completely counterintuitive for a parent to allow a child to fail. And considering all the advantages that most children born in the twenty-first century have available to them, it would appear even more difficult for them to fail. Information is at your fingertips around the clock. Technology has evolved so much that videos on virtually every topic are available to be used as a study aid in the convenience of the home. From studying for the tenth grade math regents exam to learning how to put together a bicycle—anyone can figure out how to do almost anything in this day and age. Even practicing virtual sports is available.

With all the assistance available at a moment's notice, why would anyone want to allow a child to fail? Why wouldn't a parent ensure that their child be successful in every task she took on? Isn't having a child succeed in kindergarten the first step to ensuring that she gets into a good college and then goes on to have a wonderful career? Then that wonderful career will only usher in true happiness. Right?

The question that needs to be answered is: Does recovering from failure really bring out the best in us, thereby making us more successful and happier in the end? As Kelly Clarkson sings, "What doesn't kill you makes you stronger." But this may not hold true for all of us. Looking at experiments on adults and seeing how they fare with being unsuccessful at certain times in life, it seems that not all of us will persist and succeed after facing defeat. There are always challenges that adults contend with and deciphering between the different types of failure and how adults perceive them can tells us a little about why they responded the way they did.

Henry Ford, the founder of the Ford Motor Company; Bill Gates, founder of Microsoft; Harland David Sanders, the founder of Kentucky Fried Chicken; and Walt Disney are some of the most successful business people in history, and they all have something in common. They all have a track record that included failure, sometimes multiple failures and multiple bankruptcies as well. The author of the Harry Potter series, J. K. Rowling, sent her first manuscript to twelve different publishers before one agreed to publish her work! If she did not persevere and continue on after each rejection, she would have never known the incredible success she is experiencing now.

These setbacks did not stop these giants. Why didn't they quit when they failed so miserably at times? The answer to the question is multifaceted. They were not born wanting to be ridiculously successful; however, lurking somewhere in their DNA there must be some genes that carried along their abilities to express natural talents and skills—for example, being a skilled math student, an accomplished creative writer, or having a photographic memory.

But achieving expression of some innate abilities is only the beginning to being successful. Why they didn't quit when they failed has more to do with their having learned a drive to succeed, which goes back to their childhood. The seeds were planted through obstacles that were presented to them at a young age. It is also likely that they had many life experiences that nurtured their desires to be rich and powerful, like being poor and powerless.

The past life experiences of these people shaped their prefrontal cortex to have the drive to want to win. All of our brains change in response to experiences, but the younger we are, the greater the alteration. By letting children live through failures, they literally build up the brain. The brain is like a muscle—the more we use it, the more built-up it gets. We need to be of the mind-set that teaching our kids about failing is not *failing,* but having an opportunity to work out their brain muscle and thereby build up the tracts that help them succeed. It reminds them that failure does not define who they are but will help shape who they will become.

Psychological studies show that how a person responds to defeat depends not only on the type of goal set, but also the motivation behind the goal. For instance, goals that are self-validating goals (goals that confirm a person's abilities), if met with resistance or setbacks, will inspire an individual to work harder. An example is a student applying to graduate programs or medical schools. If this student had failed at a task that was totally unrelated to their self-validating goal (i.e., becoming a doctor), they did not work harder to try to succeed at the task when given another opportunity. They did, however, persist to achieve when it was related to their self-validating goal. So, despite past childhood experiences, it appears that people have a need to persist with goals that are related to defining oneself—becoming a doctor, lawyer, poet, architect, and so forth.

Getting back to the point of why parents need to let their children falter without saving the day all the time: we know that how adults deal with daily failures and frustrations has to do with personality, individual expectation, and past learned responses. All three of these are variables that can be tinkered with to some degree.

By looking at the present we can see what went wrong or right in the past. When adults experience setbacks they rely on past experience to help them muddle through. Did the past experiences build up their ability to cope with setbacks or was their confidence shaken to the core, causing them to have fear of failure? People who have fear of failure will avoid any situation that does not guarantee success, which essentially limits their future. If one cannot venture on a quest with an unknown endpoint, that person will never have the chance to move forward. They are paralyzed individuals.

Do past failures set people up to cope better with the negative feelings that occur with poor outcomes? The memories of childhood impact our daily life. The feelings of losing a seventh-grade tennis game may come flooding back to the adult playing on the company softball team that is experiencing a defeat. The memory of the loss of the tennis game in seventh grade may have been a minor blip on the emotional radar since, way back then, the tennis coach insisted on harder practices, which ensured the next game played was a win. The life lesson learned was that trying harder made a win more likely. The adult playing in the company softball game, instead of being brought down by defeat, since he had learned a lesson from this earlier experience, is now inspired to practice to improve the odds of winning the next game. His learned response to failure was to work a little harder to improve the outcome for the next time.

But what if the feelings of losing the tennis match back in seventh grade were of overwhelming frustration, sadness, and anger? What if this constellation of emotions superseded the ability to heed the words of the coach and more intense practices did not follow? Instead of winning the next match, only more defeat followed. A cycle of negative emotions was set up with the loss of the tennis game and has perpetuated itself. Now as the adult, the same feelings of frustration and anger at the loss of the company softball game are back. There will be no plans to practice harder; just the feeling of being irritated have surfaced. This was a learned response from childhood that will continue. Part of the learned response was due to his innate personality, which did not allow him to take the advice of his coach to put more effort into practice. Now as an adult, he is responsible for any actions that follow in the wake of disappointment, but at a much bigger level.

It seems that there are many variables that have an effect on how well we cope with challenges and failures as an adult. The defeats endured as a child, along with some inherent personality traits and goals, sets up how one will respond to challenges in the future.

Now imagine a childhood that never involved a setback or failure of any kind. Think about a childhood where a parent swooped in to catch the flailing child every time there was even a possibility that the end result would not be a good one. The poor adult playing in the losing company softball game would have never had a chance to develop any coping strategy, good or bad! The emotion of losing would be a new one which, depending on the reaction, could have more severe consequences as resulting actions may jeopardize the adult's job.

The instinct of a parent is to always protect and spare the child any physical or emotional discomfort. This is a simple statement and one that most parents work very hard to ensure. For the most part this is, of course, the first rule of good parenting. Keep your kids out of physical harm's way and nurture them while giving them love and emotional support throughout life.

Unfortunately it seems that parents are taking this rule of parenting to the extreme. They are treating their child as if this precious, fragile human will implode if made to feel any miniscule type of discomfort. The mere thought of the disappointment your child will feel if he does not get a trophy for his lacrosse game or achieve the A on his math test puts a pit in your stomach. The parent feels compelled to assure that every task, from schoolwork to creative projects and sports, is a success. This is a trend that needs to be stopped!

The overprotective parent starts "catching behaviors" early on. "Catching behaviors" are the actions that intercede to make sure the child never feels uncomfortable. This can be in a physical or emotional way. Going back to the playground scenario from earlier, the over-protective parent is always within arm's reach. If the toddler starts to fall down, the parent's hand is there to lessen the fall. It is instinctual to do this, but if we are talking about letting them fall into the sand, grass, or soft plastic turf, this small fall would likely result in a scraped knee and maybe some tears. The more important point is that the toddler learned that when he fell he was able to get up again and continue to play. He learned the proverbial "If you fall, get up and keep going" lesson.

The parental reaction after these minor falls is very important. Most children do very well with minor falls; they get up and continue on. It is the parental reaction that forms how the toddler will react. A parent that rushes in with concern bordering on terror about their toddler falling sets off an emotional reaction that usually results in an escalation of crying and a continued need to be consoled for every little bump. When the toddler falls and the parent knows that no real harm occurred, it is in the best interest of the toddler to give a quick reassurance and move on. This allows the toddler to learn that falling is okay, even if it hurt a little, but getting up and continuing on is the only option.

Kids love to play games, and it is wonderful for parents to play with them. It is good bonding time for all involved. Board games are fun. For young children, playing games like Chutes and Ladders or Candy Land levels the playing field where only luck is involved in winning. No strategy or knowledge is needed. The parent playing games with the child usually lets the child win. This seems like it's a good plan of action. It's only a silly game and if little Billy wants to win he should feel the power of winning. Since the parents can't stand the thought of seeing Billy upset at losing Chutes and Ladders, they will protect their boy from feeling disappointment. After all, it is only a silly board game so what is wrong with doing this, really? It seems so natural to think the answer is "There is no harm in letting him win."

The reality is that he will win on his own at some point anyway, since the game is won by sheer luck—all you have to do is roll the dice. The parent has no advantage as far as who will win, and eventually Billy *will* win a game. But instead of waiting to let Billy win on his own, the parent throws the game to "protect" the feelings of the child. This never allows the child to experience the discomfort of losing. He does not get the chance to figure out that even though he lost the game, nothing really bad happened. He does not get the opportunity to feel that self-confidence of trying again and maybe winning the next time. He does not get the chance to feel disappointment and know that he is still safe and his parents love him. He lost a chance to learn so many things that would only serve to help him in the real world.

Let's take this lesson to the playground where little Billy is playing a game with the other kids. He starts off playing the game with robust enthusiasm, but as the game progresses he starts to realize that he is losing. He starts to feel so unnerved by the feeling of losing that he storms off the playground in a fit of rage and tears. The other young children are old enough to recognize that this is inappropriate behavior as they look at Billy with bewildered eyes. Billy was playing with his peers and they were not about to "throw" the game and let him win. His parents had him so used to winning that Billy had no idea how to handle the emotions of losing and, even worse, had to do it for the first time in front of his friends. If Billy had better parenting and they had allowed him to feel the discomfort of losing, he would have had a marvelous time playing on the playground with his friends and then gone on to play a second game for a chance at redemption.

The pattern of protection continues on as fear of failure grows more intensely in parents of school-age children. The child not only has school to contend with, but sports and a social life as well. There are so many areas where the over-protective parent swoops in to catch the child. The parent makes sure every homework assignment is done to perfection before being handed in. They grill the child before each test and when doing school projects, not only do they help; they end up doing most of the project. They are intervening all the time when things are going well. Now throw in a failing grade in a class. Running up to the school to confront the teacher and demand a better grade since your child deserves to pass "just for working hard," is not helping. The lesson learned by the child is that if we kick and scream hard enough we will get what we want. It is like reinforcing a temper tantrum in the toddler. Parents do this all the time when they feel the need to protect their child from feeling the discomfort of failing.

But what the parent needs to do is understand that the discomfort will more likely induce the child to work harder and be smarter the next quarter. It is okay to sometimes fail! This is the take away message that the child must learn. Ask them how they could have done things differently? What did they do or not do that resulted in the failing grade? What will they do the next time to prevent this from happen? All this is an invaluable learning experience.

Most of us don't like the feeling of failing, and we will most certainly try to avoid it. We develop strategies to aggressively avoid failing, whether it's working harder to improve study skills, using the extra help offered after school, or prioritizing time better. Give your child the opportunity to learn this life lesson. It will never happen if you save the day all the time. You cannot and should not be around at all times to ensure the success of your child.

Today's society has become focused on making sure that children feel as if they are winners all of the time. School tournaments give out trophies to all the children who participate, whether they win or lose, so everyone can feel like a winner and there are no hurt feelings. We have to ask ourselves: what is this really doing to our kids? They will discover as they get older that only one person or team can come out on top and only that person or team should have the honor of a trophy.

Children need to learn that it is fine to not always be on top and win all the time. Parents may inherently believe this for themselves, but it is much harder to see your child flounder and fail and to resist aggressively intervening on their behalf.

Instead of constantly intervening, you should allow things to take their course and continue to praise your child for participating and practicing and working hard. In reality, these are the traits that will make your child a success in life anyway.

This approach is easier if you remind yourself that a child who is never allowed to experience defeat loses out on some profound life lessons. A tendency to continually catch your children before they fall will not allow them to understand how to deal with defeat, how to push themselves to work harder, or how to feel humility. These life lessons serve to make a more productive, happy, and empathetic adult. The bottom line is that letting a child fail does more to teach her how to succeed then letting her win all the time.

Step 4

Be the Boss

Mother is a verb. It's something you do. Not just who you are.

Cheryl Lacey Donovan
The Ministry of Motherhood

- *Ask only one time—your voice becomes silent to your children if you repeatedly have to ask for something to get done*

- *Establish boundaries and expectations of behavior*

- *When you say no, you should stick to your decision*

- *Avoid the "omnipotent parent syndrome"*

Today's parents are absolutely terrified that every move they make, if not done correctly, will have long lasting and potentially psychologically damaging effects on their children. The parent who asks for help because their eighteen-month-old does not sleep through the night rejects the advice to just let him "cry it out for a few nights" because of the fear of inflicting lasting psychological harm.

Despite the intellectually obvious reality that the baby is in a loving, comfortable, and safe environment, the parent is overwhelmed by the fear that they are causing great distress to their baby, which may, in turn, cause a child's future feelings of abandonment. They can't possibly let the baby cry it out. Instead they feel safer sticking to their plan of rocking the baby to sleep each night and to get up to do this during the multiple times the baby wakes up throughout the night. The parent has willingly relinquished control to an eighteen-month-old baby and has no qualms about it!

Are we raising a generation of children who cannot and will not handle "no"? Why are parents giving control to children? In a recent poll, about 80 percent of parents felt their children were spoiled. This obviously says more about ineffective parenting than it does about the children. It is hard to admit this, and time after time parents who feel they have done their best throw up their hands in exasperation asking, "But what did I do wrong?"

At least there is recognition that maybe the upbringing did promulgate this undesired outcome. Children are, after all, a product of their surroundings, and if parents apparently are not providing the proper grounds for growing up, we can't blame the kids. The onus must fall on the parents.

What is going on that has caused this phenomenon of "spoiling" their children to become so common among parents today? What has caused the paradigm of good parenting to shift to, "Whatever you want my love, I am here to please you."

Perhaps it started with the idea that it was better to parent with a softer hand, as Dr. Spock advised us in the late forties. He advised parents to "trust yourself" and wanted parents to move away from the hard line of strict rules. He suggested *appropriately* that parents show affection to their children instead of following the misguided advice that showing a child affection made them "weak." He urged parents to hug their kids and tell them they are "loved, unique, and special." He wanted parents to allow their children to express themselves and urged parents to move away from spanking. Instead parents were advised to use their verbal skills to discipline the children (hitting children is always a bad idea).

Dr. Spock was ahead of his time with his ideas on parenting. His ideas that the parents know best and the "trust your instinct" advice were insightful for his time. His original book has changed over the years but the basic premise has stayed the same. However, it is quite possible that the pendulum has swung too far in the direction of parents allowing their children's emotions to have too much influence over how they raise their kids. They have crossed the line of being the benevolent ruler who cares for the baby with love yet disciplines firmly, to parents that are concerned with the damage that might be inflicted if little Blake is disappointed that his birthday party did not have a plethora of balloons for decoration.

Today's parents seem over the top with worry that placing too many demands on their child may cause emotional stress and bring on anxiety. This is coming from an already anxiety-ridden parent. Worry begets worry in a family. Their worry about being an omnipotent parent in the world of their child is paralyzing good sense about how to raise them. I call this the "omnipotent parent syndrome."

This happens when a parent is in a chronic state of worry and feeling that any disciplinary action that is made in raising a child is going to have everlasting negative effects on them. It becomes a near impossible task to bring up a child with boundaries. Imagine the burden for young parents having to worry that saying no to their child may crush their independent spirit and wither away their ego? How is it possible to raise a child in this anxiety-filled environment? It's time to take a new trajectory!

So what does being the boss mean? It means setting limits and giving boundaries to your children. It means telling them no and really meaning "no" as opposed to "maybe" or "let me think about it for a while" or "if you carry on enough I will change my mind." It should be only on a very rare occasion that you bend to this behavior. If your child starts to whine, and you change your mind and give in out of sheer exhaustion, you are reinforcing the behavior of "if I object and complain I get what I want," and that is far from the desired effect we want when we are drawing a line.

Frequently it is so much easier to give them what they want, especially after a long day at work when the parent is tired and worn down. The last thing they want is to hear their child start to cry and have a tantrum over not getting their way. It is easier to just give in. This is very shortsighted on the part of the parent. The behavior of whining and tantrums will be reinforced, and this is how your child learns to manipulate you to get what he desires. Parents cannot afford to be shortsighted, not only for their own sake, but for the sake of their child.

The boundary is the imaginary line that can't be crossed. It is a set of rules that must be followed. Setting up boundaries is akin to setting up a playing field for the kids. They know where they can play and where the out-of-bounds area is. Children who are given boundaries feel much safer and know what to expect. They know exactly what they can and can't do, which feels much more secure and comfortable than not knowing what is expected of them. The feeling of being able to do whatever they please is not a good feeling for children. They thrive on boundaries, limitations, and guidelines, and when raised within this framework fare much better than children who are not reared this way.

Families that provide boundaries raise children who are much less likely to act out and rebel. Children without clear boundaries are more apt to develop risk-taking behaviors and have a harder time playing with friends and taking turns. They are too used to having their needs gratified instantly and, as a result, don't want to wait their turn when with other children. Their internal disorganization manifests as these behaviors.

Setting limits with babies is probably the easiest and hardest task at the same time. The parent has the ability to be in complete control over the baby, but is either too worried or too emotionally overtaken to set up a good set of guidelines. Their difficulty with setting limits stems from two main areas: their worry that it may have long-lasting damaging effects on the baby, and the parental desire to satisfy a basic internal need.

In my practice, the most talked about subject when it comes to babies is sleep. Setting limits when it comes to sleeping makes everyone's life so much better. Putting the baby to sleep without any help from something they associate with bedtime and sleeping, such as a pacifier, bottle, music wheel, or the necessity of your singing a lullaby or rocking them, is the first boundary you will set with your child. You establish with them that the way we go to sleep is not dependent on these sleeping aids or your provision of these rituals.

The baby should always be put into the crib when he is still awake. This is a key component of the routine of going to bed. This allows the baby to develop his own mechanisms of soothing. A bedtime routine of bathing, reading books, and quiet time is a wonderful prequel to being put into the crib for the night. If this is started early on, bedtime will be much easier.

If a parent has not set limits for sleeping habits and the baby is running the nighttime routine, this can still be undone. Implement the guidelines of putting the baby into the crib awake so he can start to learn the self-soothe mechanisms. If needed, a parent can go in periodically to give a smile and words of encouragement, "Mommy is here, but it is night and bedtime." Waiting longer and longer periods of time until the parent goes back in the room will allow more time for the baby to try to learn to self-soothe. If we don't let him cry a bit he won't ever be given the opportunity to lull himself to sleep.

Parents will often say, "You don't understand, Doctor, my baby has the most intense cry and never stops; he can cry *all* night. It is not possible to let him cry it out." Or "That does not work for my baby. He just never stops crying." When asked to give a little more detail about what is happening at night, the parent usually confesses that he was unable to let his baby cry for more than twenty minutes at a time and eventually rocks him to sleep or takes him back to the parent's bed. Many parents, despite being rational, intelligent people, think their child is the special child who will not be able to thrive if given boundaries for going to bed at night.

Similar limits apply to waking up in the morning. It is the parental job to decide when the day starts and when to take the baby out of the crib. If your day starts at 7:00 a.m., that is the time the baby is taken out of the crib. If she gets up at 5:00 a.m., you need to let her know that the day has not started in the household yet. (This applies to older babies who are big enough to sleep twelve hours without feeding.)

This is not mean and the baby won't have feelings of abandonment. If the baby is raised in a loving, caring home, setting sleep boundaries is only going to be helpful to the whole household. If she wakes up early, she can play and roll around and sing and talk to herself in the crib, but it is not time to start the day, and she should not be taken out of the crib. It is much easier to do this when the baby is young as opposed to accomplishing this with the talking, cajoling, bargaining toddler, who is calling you four or five times throughout the night to tell you "Mommy I need you, Mommy. I need water!" It is up to the parent to set the rules for sleeping and stick to them (assuming the baby is healthy of course).

Once babies become toddlers, they will start to explore the environment by touching and attempting to manipulate everything. Some are still using their mouths to explore and help them figure out the world, and yet their ability to physically and mentally move in the world around them has started. Their instant needs gratification is in full swing: they see something and they want it immediately. The toddler who goes to put his hand onto the hot stove must be taught, "No, that's hot! You will get a boo-boo," to avoid bodily harm. A walk in the park with the toddler who picks up the duck poop must result in him being immediately told, "No that is yucky," or else cautiously steering him away from the water's edge with the gentle reminder, "That's dangerous." These kinds of boundaries to establish what is safe are easy to set, and most parents have no problem enforcing them. The toddler has the playing field laid out pretty quickly: no touching of hot stoves or electrical outlets, no stepping on the dog, or eating dirt.

Starting to set the boundaries for other issues that don't involve safety offers up a much bigger challenge. Saying no to the toddler can and often does set off a cascade of tears, sulking, and sad faces that brings a parent to their knees. Stay strong as you move through this phase. It is very important to set up strong boundaries. As you lay them out you may be amazed to see how your little toddler loves nothing more than to follow rules. He might not like being told, "It is time to clean up the blocks," but will soon feel satisfied and pleased with himself for following the command to please his parent as you praise this process. A child will like hearing "You listened so well and worked hard to put your toys away."

If the toddler is a typical child, you can be sure he is going to do his job to test the limits of what is allowed multiple times a day. A mom or dad can feel like they spend their whole existence sniping at them, "No honey don't touch that," or "No you can't watch television." It can be an endless cacophony of "No, no, no." This can be frustrating to the toddler since that may be all they are hearing as the limits are being determined.

There are ways to put a more positive spin on the boundary setting that can make things more pleasant. It is possible to use yes words and still say no.

For example if your toddler is insisting on wanting to go outside to play ball just as the family is sitting to have dinner, a reply akin to, "Yes! We can play ball, but first let us sit and eat dinner." Or the toddler who wants to wear his winter coat in the summertime can be told, "Yes, we can wear the coat when it is colder outside. But we will wear this today." This should be less trying for the parent, since a positive spin is often a good angle to take with the toddler. They feel as if they are getting something even in the face of the "no" answer. If this technique does not always work and results in a tantrum, it is still important to stick to your answer and try this positive spin on another occasion.

A common source of struggle that parents face with toddlers is getting them to eat in a healthy way. It is often surprising to see how many toddlers are in charge of their food intake. It is not unusual to hear a parent complain, "My son eats nothing but chicken nuggets and mac and cheese. He refuses to eat anything else!" The solution to this problem is simple. Stop giving him chicken nuggets and mac and cheese! There is not a toddler in this universe capable of getting into a car and driving somewhere to grab some chicken nuggets from Wendy's. The parent is in charge of the food they give their toddler.

Why do parents feel that it is okay to let a twenty-eight-month-old make the decisions about what food they can eat? One of the most important rules a parent can follow when it comes to eating is remembering that they must supply the food choices, and then the child can select which ones they want and how much they want.

Never, ever, make food an issue to be fought over, and never make your child finish his food. Make healthy food choices for dinner, and make only one dinner for the whole family. You are not a full-time cook committed to supplying separate meals for each child based on their palate. You make a meal, and if they don't like what is served for dinner, then they don't need to eat. It's quite fine if a child does not eat a meal when offered food. Parents are riddled with worry that if they are not supplying the requested macaroni and cheese, the child will go to bed hungry. A healthy child will never willingly starve if food is available, so offer up only healthy choices and you will gain back control.

A reminder here is to keep the junk food out of the house so it is not an option to fight over. For example, if your thirty-month-old son refuses to eat the salmon and kale chip dinner you made, but sees there are chocolate chip cookies on the counter, a real battle is going to start. That shouldn't be a food choice available in the house. Only healthy foods should be available, so if they refuse the dinner that you made and cry that they are hungry, you can offer up some other ready alternative, like cut up vegetables. This does not require any work and is an okay alternative that does not require a parent to cook another meal.

Parents need to take a step back from their worry that their child may go hungry. It is okay if they start to cry and scream, "I want chicken nuggets for dinner! I'm not eating this!" If you remain calm and a bit removed emotionally, your children will accept your staying in control of the choices available. A little less worry and some limits on food choices goes a long way toward doing your best as a parent.

The preschooler years offer more of a challenge to your being the boss since their verbal skills are skyrocketing and every decision may end up in an attempted bargaining session. As they are sent out into the world with other children, they must learn to delay their need for instant gratification of their desires. The boundaries need to be very clear at this time. It is not okay if Randi goes to nursery school and decides she wants Lenny's lollipop and takes it out of his hand. The preschooler must understand the boundary of other people's properties, and the school setting gives the ultimate test. The setting of limits should have started at home, as it is not acceptable for your children to be taking or playing with anyone's toys unless given explicit permission. If this was made clear in your household, this attitude should easily transfer to the school setting.

This is also the time where parents start setting the limits on acceptable language and how to use pleasing phrases like "thank-you" and "you're welcome." Letting your child know what behaviors are acceptable to you and others helps them to have a positive outlook on life. You can encourage their good behaviors with a smile and a "praise the process" phrase like, "I like how you used those nice words." Never tell a child he or she is "bad." You don't want to set up a constant negative input that can result in a self-fulfilling prophecy. Convey to them that it is the action that is bad, not the child.

Being the boss does not always have to involve saying, "No don't do that." A person in charge can be just as effective when saying, "Do this instead." It is better to tell your preschool child what to do rather than what not to do when they are pushing the boundaries. For instance, if Bobby is recurrently pulling the cat's tail, a parent will get a lot further by saying in a calm quiet voice, "Bobby, petting Fluffy is what we do to him, and he really loves it!" If the parent reacts with a boisterous, "No Bobby! Don't do that to Fluffy!" he might be getting the exact response he wants from the parent, which is immediate and loud attention. If Bobby insists on throwing his blocks he can be gently told, "We use the blocks for building fun things, Bobby, how about building a castle?" The quiet, calm approach with a positive spin is always the better path to take to setting the limits.

If the child does not respond to this positive approach and insists on pushing a boundary that has been drawn, there needs to be an immediate consequence to this behavior. This may consist of a time-out (the number of minutes corresponding to their years of age), the toy being taken away, or the child being removed from the situation. The sooner your child knows that his mom and dad mean what they say and that he is responsible for following the rules that have been set up, the happier everyone will be.

A reminder here: don't let yourself be in a position where you have accidently put your child in the driver's seat. Parents may unwittingly give their child the opportunity to be in control and be defiant. This happens when a parent makes a request of the child like "Hug Aunt Phoebe and tell her you love her," or "Give Grandma a kiss." These are commands given to a child that can be refused outright, and there is very little a parent can do to make these things happen. You can't force your child to give someone a hug or a high five or utter the words "I love you" if they don't want to.

What usually happens is that a few requests are made and the child refuses to do as the parent wishes. Since it is the child's prerogative not to give someone a kiss or hug, this is not a situation where their disregard for your request should end in a punishment. However, the takeaway message for the child is they can refuse your request without a consequence. The better tactical approach to these types of situations is to ask the child, "Would you like to give Aunt Phoebe a kiss?" "Would you like to give Grandma a kiss?" This takes the control out of the child's hands since you are merely asking a question and not giving a command. The question only requires a yes or no response and does not put the child in the position of outwardly disobeying a parental request. The child will than make the decision without having been put in a position of power.

Time flies by when you are raising your children, and before you know it you have a grade-school child. Once the child is in school, the limits have exponentially risen, but hopefully the groundwork was laid out from the beginning. The expectations of the school-age child include getting up for school, going to school, following the rules and regulations of the school, doing chores, and respecting adults and peers.

The regulations in the household should stay strong as life gets busier and the outside world takes on a bigger influence in the life of your child. There must be limits set on television and computer time as well as video game time. The child is responsible for getting up and getting ready for school at a set time and the appropriate time to go to bed should also be adhered to. Effective and respectful communication on the part of the child needs to be reinforced with appropriate follow-through if he is crossing a line.

These limits are all well intended, but hard to maintain if you do not set out to reinforce them. The school-age child will continue to push each boundary, especially if they sense any bit of hesitancy in a parent. Continue on with the rules, and don't back down, no matter how hard the child pushes back. If they see your weakness, they have garnered control, and this makes the parent's job much harder.

Telling your nine-year-old daughter to go brush her teeth and stop playing video games on a school night means she must do as you requested. If you set up a time for bed each night, she should be aware of the set time and should not be surprised by this request. A common problem is that the child does not listen on the first request and the parent again needs to remind her. This may happen three or four times before the parent gets fed up and starts to raise their voice in complete and utter aggravation. Sometimes the raised voice does not work to get more of a response. The child may stop playing the video game and brush their teeth, but then instead of going to bed, goes to watch television. The child followed through on half of the request, so they feel they deserve something more.

The feeling of not being in control of your own child and then losing control by yelling and screaming is not at all pleasant, and is unfortunately all too common. Children that must be told to do something multiple times in order to get a response have essentially become deaf to the parental voice, likely because there have been no consequences for failure to do what was asked of them. When you make a request to a child, especially when they are engaged in a consuming activity, make sure they heard you. Do this by saying, "Carissa, look at me for a second." Make sure you have eye contact before you make your request so there is no backtracking by saying, "But Mom, I didn't hear you!"

By ensuring you have eye contact you are making sure they heard you or at least were aware that you wanted to communicate with them. If there is no response to your command, it is very reasonable to dole out a consequence immediately and calmly. "Carissa I asked you five minutes ago to stop playing video games, brush your teeth, and go to bed. You didn't listen to me so there will be a consequence." At this point, chances are very great that she is going to make her case as to why she didn't listen to you. "Mom, it's too early for bed," or "Mom, I didn't hear you," or "Please Mom, let me stay up a little longer, I did all my homework and I am such a great student, come on Mom, I deserve to play longer!"

Whatever potential argument comes out of her mouth, don't get sidetracked from the problem. She didn't respond to you when you asked. This is the boundary that was set and it must be followed. The much bigger picture here is the child's belief that it is okay to ignore mom or dad since they don't really have power. Be the boss!

It is so helpful for children to have parents who rule with compassion and who quietly but determinedly follow through. Everyone knows what to expect at all times and there aren't any surprises. If Carissa's routine each night includes being told seventeen times to stop playing video games with her dad finally physically shutting off the video game, it would not be fair if one night her dad starts screaming at her to "do as you are told."

We can't expect certain actions from our children if the path is not laid out correctly. In this scenario, once the parent is aware that there was no response from the child, the consequence for this behavior needs to be stated immediately. "Since you didn't do as I asked the first time, I am taking away video game time for tomorrow and it will be easier to go to bed tomorrow night." The parent must decide the appropriate consequence to ensure that next time, when a request is made, the child follows through. In other words, the consequence must have meaning. If you use a consequence like, "You're not going to sleep over at Grandma's house next week," but you know that your child does not get very excited about a Grandma's house sleepover, it is an ineffectual consequence.

A parent may use these types of consequences that are easier to dole out with less likelihood of a fallout with crying and hysterics. But if a parent uses ineffectual consequences, don't expect to see results. The consequences must have meaning and evoke an emotional response in the child. Remember again to always remain calm and in control, especially when giving out the consequence of a transgression. If you are feeling exceptionally angry, it is not unreasonable to wait five or ten minutes to calm down and give out an appropriate consequence with a calm demeanor.

The old saying "Pick your battles," is good advice during the school-age era, but this does not mean backing down on rules that have been set already. The rules that apply to school, chores, being respectful, health, and media screen time should be set rules with certain limits in place. Some other unimportant, less pressing issues that may arise can be talked about with the child as long as they know that no matter what your decision is, it sticks.

A milder issue may arise if, for example, your child comes home and wants to dye her hair since "All the girls are doing it." This is a scenario where there were no ground rules established, so there may be some leeway allowed. It is not unreasonable to talk with the child about the desire to change her hair color. This is a temporary change and you may give the child the opportunity to give reasons why it should be allowed. It must be conveyed that, as a parent, you are willing to listen to their desire, but ultimately it is your decision and they must abide by it.

Once the parent has thought about the issue and made the decision, there is no backing down. That is it. No cajoling, begging, or bribery on the child's part should change your mind. Giving the child the opportunity to speak her mind and then taking adequate time to make a decision is a very reasonable approach when dealing with special requests and situations.

Other minor issues may involve a parent's distress over clothing that they deem unacceptable. An example is a nine-year-old boy, Peter, who insists on wearing the same two or three outfits over and over again. The father is quite perturbed by his son, who only likes to wear sweatpants and golf shirts to school. The father prefers that he wear a button-down shirt with zipper pants, especially since he has a closet full of nice clothes. The father refuses to let his son go to school each day in sweatpants, despite the fact that they don't violate the school's dress code. This has made Peter resentful since every other kid in school wears sweatpants and golf shirts. Peter has become angry and depressed because several of his friends have commented on how he is dressed differently.

It is important to throw this reminder at parents: This is a minor issue and does not need to be controlled by the parent as long as the clothes are clean and decent. Stressing that the clothes are clean and decent should be the rule set down that must be adhered to. These comfort clothes do not need to be a source of contention between parent and child, as this is not an important issue. Stick to important issues, especially as the kids get older. There is no reason to be arguing over unimportant topics like how your son wants to assert his style of clothing, or how your daughter wants to wear her hair. These are safe, nonthreatening ways that children use to assimilate with their peers. Fitting in and going with the trends, as long as they are safe, should at least be talked about with an open mind. Try to remember when you were a kid how important it was to have the haircut that was in style. As the benevolent dictator in the household, having good judgment and remaining the boss in control of things that matter is what is important.

As the teenage years approach, social life will be at the forefront of your child's existence. This is what is expected and should be encouraged, to an extent. Their world revolves around their friends, and they are very concerned with how they are viewed by them. They want to fit in and see their friends as being closer to them than their own family. The input of friends carries more weight than their parent's advice at this time of life. The adolescent will start to feel as if the parent knows little in comparison to how much knowledge they have. After all they are the ones in school doing all the learning!

Now is the time when pushing the boundaries gets a little more intense. Being in control as a parent is increasingly more important. Keep calm, don't lose your temper, and don't let your feelings of frustration take over. Once you have lost control and start screaming and yelling, you have given the power to your adolescent. You have given them access to your hot button, since they now know how to upset you. That can be a dangerous situation!

The adolescent child is now out doing after-school activities, attending clubs and sports, and spends more time outside the home than inside. As they are starting their movement toward more independence, there begins as well the internal struggle within themselves of needing their parents and not wanting to need them. This can create a bit of or a lot of disharmony if the right groundwork was not laid down.

If you are the parent who tells your adolescent, "Clean your room before going to your friend's house," and then lets him off the hook without a consequence for not doing this, be prepared for some rocky roads ahead. If clear boundaries were not set up and the adolescent has free roaming access, the pushing of limits is going to come to a head. Every adolescent has a doctoral degree in how to stretch the rules, and now it is most important to make sure the lines are well delineated.

The area of respectful communication established when they are young has its earliest seeds of breaking down in the adolescent years, and it is imperative that mutual respect between parent and child stays strong. It is normal for the adolescent to think they may know more than the parent, but this does not give them a pass to be disrespectful. A clear-cut boundary should be spelled out on how you expect your adolescent to speak to you.

An example is fifteen-year-old Riley, who comes home with a friend after his soccer game. They are in the kitchen looking for food, since they just played a tough game and want to eat. "Hey Ma, what is there to eat?" The kitchen is well stocked and his mother replies, "We have so much food, Riley, look in the fridge and take what you want." Riley responds "Ma, what the hell, can't you make something for us? My friend is here. I don't want to waste time making something."

Many parents can relate to this scenario continuing in this manner: "Riley, last I checked you have two hands, so you can make it yourself even if you have a friend over." "Holy shit Ma, are you kidding me? Can't you just make us some grilled cheese sandwiches or something?" So the line was crossed. Riley is pushing the limits by cursing and treating his mother poorly by not respecting her. While cursing is not the worst habit an adolescent can pick up, there should be some limits set about this. It is hard to stop an adolescent from cursing, but it should be expected that they don't curse at you.

Treating his mother and other family members with respect should be demanded. This is a nonnegotiable issue. Being rude must be followed with a consequence, and it should happen close to the moment of the bad behavior. These types of scenes are often ignored so as not to embarrass the adolescent. The parent feels too uncomfortable bringing up the obvious offense, but the adolescent won't learn not to do this in the future if you wait to reprimand him when it is "safe." Call him out on the behavior in front of his friend in a nonconfrontational manner.

This may make him feel uncomfortable—and that is exactly what you want. He does not want to be reprimanded in front of his friends, and he will learn that he stepped out of bounds.

Setting limits as far as curfews, alcohol and drug use, and driving are crucial boundaries that need to be spelled out clearly. Absolutely no blurred lines or wishy-washy parenting about this! The natural curiosity and social aspect of adolescence fosters the interest in experimenting with alcohol and drugs. If you have raised a child who has had little setting of limits up until this time, it is imperative that you get your game on. Your child's life may depend on it. If you set the curfew at 10:00 p.m. and your child shows up at 11:00 p.m., an appropriate consequence must follow. It is not enough to just say you're upset or yell at them. There are times when it might be out of the hands of the adolescent; e.g., the parent who was supposed to pick them up showed up late. In that case allowances can be made. Otherwise if they don't follow your rules, there must be a penalty.

Alcohol and drug use among adolescents is a huge problem. There must be clear lines as to what is acceptable and what is not. The lines cannot be blurred and it is at this time that kids need a strong parent more than ever. They can't be left to flounder on their own, or else there is a good chance that a catastrophe will happen. Ruling with a strong sense of direction is what the adolescent needs; even if he does not want it, he will thank you later.

Try not to get into a mode where your empathy takes over good sense. This may happen when you are feeling the disappointment your child is feeling as a result of a punitive action. This is not an unusual situation and may cause you to bend a boundary unnecessarily. For example, your sixteen-year-old daughter Margret comes home from her friend's house intoxicated for the second time. The first time she returned home from this friend's house in an intoxicated state, she was let off with a verbal warning reiterating the limits on underage drinking. This time, unfortunately, she spends most of the night vomiting from the alcohol and then sleeps most of the next day.

As a parent, you are sick with worry, but relieved to know she is okay the next day. You went through the cycle of emotions: angry she disobeyed you and drank alcohol to excess, scared she was so ill from it, and finally relieved to see she was okay. Now is the time to give out a punishment, since she was instructed not to drink alcohol and blatantly stepped out of bounds. As a parent you want this consequence to be significant, so you decide that she is no longer allowed to go to this friend's house. After all, this is the second time she had access to large amounts of alcohol there.

The next party that rolls around turns out to be a huge birthday party at this same friend's house, but it is off-limits as a result of the consequence you gave out. Your daughter is terribly upset and is sitting in her room sulking because "Half the high school is gonna be there and I can't go." Most parents will feel their daughter's pain, but if you make a decision and set a limit, it is not a good idea to back down, however hard this may be. Margret will get over not going to the birthday party and will have learned that her parents are limit setters and will follow through on the consequences if rules are not adhered to. If the parent becomes too empathetic to their child's pain and backs down because of worry that their daughter is suffering, they become ineffectual. The next time their daughter wants to get out of a consequence determined for inappropriate behavior, all she has to do is act upset and sulk.

A day in the pediatrician's office can be very telling as to the milieu of child rearing. Take a typical day in an office. The first appointment is for a four-year-old who comes in with his mom for a rash. Colton is a talkative, adorable blue-eyed boy sitting on the exam table with his mom in the chair next to the table. He did not jump off the table or immediately cry for his mom when the doctor walked in—good signs so far that he is confident or at least able to control his fear at being in the doctor's office. Maybe it is his innate nature or maybe the parent is doing something right at home by having expectations as to how Colton is required to act. He is quite cooperative during the exam; he responds to commands like open your mouth without hesitancy. He is a pleasing young man, who is calm even in the face of being in the scary doctor's office. All in all it's a good visit up until the inquiry of whether Colton should get a flu shot.

Flu season is on the way, and the doctor suggests that Colton needs his flu vaccine. In this scenario, it is up to the parent to make the decision. But Colton's mom did not agree. She turned to Colton and said, "Colton, do you want a flu shot?" He immediately starts to scream, "No, no, no, no shot, Ma, I don't want a shot!" He flies off the table and starts to run for the door. No four-year-old willingly agrees to a shot, so why would a parent put this burden on a child? Poor Colton is terrified, not just because of the possibility of getting a shot, but because his little mind cannot handle the pressure of making a medical decision! Colton does not have the ability to decipher the meaning of getting vaccinated. The message that Colton is getting is, "I am in control," and it is horrifying.

Children thrive on boundaries, and he does not want to be in charge. He is too young to take on the responsibility of this decision. So why did his mom so inappropriately throw the ball in Colton's court? Why did she involve him in the decision-making process? Her previous parenting idea was to allow Colton to be involved in decisions so he feels important. She also did not want the responsibility of upsetting Colton with a shot. She was worried about him being upset by the millisecond pinch he would feel getting the shot and then being angry with her for allowing this to happen. She was fearful of his anger. If Colton's mom does not please him all the time, she fears he will not love her. She has become someone afflicted with "omnipotent parent syndrome." His being upset by her decision to give him a vaccine and upset him momentarily might have everlasting effects on him. The reality of living in a privileged atmosphere and having access to excellent medical care does not factor into her irrational fear of having the omnipotent parent syndrome.

The pediatrician uses this opportunity to remind the mother that it is not appropriate to let a four-year-old make a decision regarding his health, but they walk out of the office without the shot.

Time to move on to the next patient. Michelle is a ten-year-old girl in for a checkup. The doctor walks into the room to find that Michelle and her mom are having a heated exchange. The mother turns to the doctor and says, "My gosh, Doctor, can you do something to help me with her? She has such a fresh mouth, I swear I am not going to survive the next few years." Michelle turns to her mother and says, "Oh Ma, please shut up! You're such a pain." With that the mother replies, "Do you see what I have to put up with? In my day, my mother would have smacked me if I said that to her!" The doctor inquires as to the nature of the spat. Michelle says that she wants to be able to go to a Friday night coed party, and her mom is attempting to say no.

This is an all too common scene, as the preadolescents try to assert themselves and have more independence. However, if the right foundation of boundaries and limit setting were not enforced early on, the preadolescent is going to easily railroad the parent. Michelle is very used to getting her way and has no fear of the consequences of being so blatantly rude to her mother, because there haven't been any in the past. The doctor asks Michelle, "Why would you tell your mother to shut up?" Michelle replies, "You don't understand how mean she is; she doesn't trust me enough to let me go to this party!"

The banter goes back and forth until the exam is over. Michelle has clearly not been taught how to speak to her mother, or at least has not had a consequence for doing this that meant something to her. Once Michelle starts to use words like "shut up" directed at her mother, the conversation is over, and whatever it is that Michelle was fighting for should be immediately taken off the table as a punishment for her actions. This effective, swift, and calm reaction to her stepping out of bounds will go a very long way in teaching her how to speak to her mom in the future.

The next room is a sick visit with two siblings in tow. The room is in complete chaos as the doctor walks in. One of the kids, a six-year-old named Aaron, is sitting on the doctor's stool spinning it around, while the other, four-year-old Adam, is precariously playing with the doctor's equipment. The equipment is kept out of the children's reach, which means someone handed it to him or he climbed up to retrieve it. The mother is not saying a word to stop the children from potentially getting hurt and falling off the spinning stool or damaging the equipment. The poor little sick sibling feels too ill to move and is lying on the table, causing no trouble.

The mom politely asks Adam to give the doctor the equipment back but he refuses, "I want to play with it Mom." The mother becomes more insistent saying, "*Please* give it to the doctor." Adam continues to ignore his mom, so his mother's voice grows more annoyed, "If you don't give it back to the doctor *now*, you are not getting any dessert tonight." Adam is feeling the potential threat of not getting his dessert, but he forges on and continues to ignore his mom. With that, the mother rips the equipment out of his hand and angrily squeezes his arm while pulling him onto her lap.

Adam starts to cry and throws himself onto the floor in a fit of anger. Aaron quickly gets off the spinning chair as he watches his mother grow angry for fear he will be grabbed next. In this scenario, Adam was used to getting what he wanted and didn't fear the consequence of not getting his dessert. First and foremost, any punishment at this young age needs to be quick and swift, not deferred until later. The four-year-old won't even remember why he is not getting dessert that evening, so if you want to dole out a punishment to a little child, do it in the moment to make it more effective.

Secondly, Adam's mom was essentially talking to the wall since she had to ask him three times, and even after the third time he still didn't listen. The only way she was able to achieve success was to lose her temper and get physical with him. She has ineffectual parenting skills. Being the boss means you only ask once. There is no next time. By expecting a child to respond to you the first time you make a demand, you are laying the groundwork that you are in charge and consequences will occur if you are not listened to. *Your voice becomes silent to your children if you repeatedly have to ask for something to get done.*

Once you have to yell at a child you have lost control, and in a sense they have won. It is always easier said than done when it comes to kids, but these are habits that you can start early. From the day they start to understand language, you can start to give commands and have expectations for them. Always remain in control and never ever use any sort of physical punishment.

In this scenario, if Adam didn't listen the first time, the mom should gently take the instrument out of his hands and give it to the doctor. The crying and tantrum would likely follow immediately after, and then it is important to remember to never respond to a tantrum unless the child is in real physical danger, such as running in a parking lot. He will throw himself on the floor and bang his head, but don't worry, he won't hurt himself. A common parental mistake is to rush in and try to console the child or worry that he will hurt himself as he bangs his head and fists on the floor.

Children will not willingly hurt themselves in a tantrum, but if you are really worried you can pick him up and carry him to a carpeted room without talking to him. Parents should be cognizant of accidently giving secondary reinforcement to the tantrum by trying to cajole them out of one or asking how you can make it better. No parent wants to see their child in such misery that they are writhing and screaming on the floor, but resist that urge to swoop in and help them. They will help themselves and eventually calm down.

Once the tantrum has receded and he is quiet, this is the time to praise the process of how your son was able to calm down on his own. If Adam did not go into a tantrum and accepted that his mom took away the equipment, there should be a follow-through on the fact that Adam didn't listen the first time he was asked. This takes a lot of work! Many parents are too tired, or it is not the right time and place to give a punishment, but is there really ever the correct time and place to discipline a child? These situations happen every day and parents need to make them learning scenarios or else the opportunity is lost. When the child realizes that you are the boss, these scenarios will happen very infrequently as they will do what you say when you say it.

Moving through the scenes of a day in a pediatrician's office, in the next room is twenty-three-month-old Simon, who has a diaper rash. His wonderfully sweet parents are with him and terribly concerned about his bad diaper rash. "Doctor, we are having such a problem with him. He won't let us change his diaper, so we are picking our battles and are changing it less frequently. Now he has a rash." The doctor is a bit confused and asks, "What do you mean he won't let you change his diaper?"

"He won't let us change his diaper." The pediatrician is still confused and inquires, "Do you ask his permission before you change him?" The parents respond with an abject, "No, of course not."

"Then what is the problem here? Simon is a twenty-six-pound toddler and you two are grown adults. I don't see how he doesn't let you change the diaper."

"Oh, Doctor, you would not believe how he fights us and how upset he gets, so we are doing it less often so we don't upset him as much."

Here we have two adults letting the twenty-three-month-old decide whether he will allow his diaper to be changed or not. Simon is in control because it is too upsetting to the parent to see him fight and cry. Common sense is flying out the window and the omnipotent parent syndrome is taking over, as they fear that there is going to be some long-lasting psychological damage because Simon didn't want to have his diaper changed and his parents insisted it had to be done.

It is okay if his parents have to struggle a bit with Simon as they gently hold him down to change him. He will realize that his parents are in control. Be the boss. It's easy. By changing his diaper, the parents are merely taking care of him. They are keeping him clean and healthy, not hurting him. The worry over his crying has left the parents partially paralyzed, allowing him to stay in dirty diapers and worsening the diaper rash.

Onto the next room where there are three girls waiting; the oldest child is home. Since only three are in the office, the doctor inquires as to the whereabouts of the oldest girl, Donna. "She is home making dinner for us." The pediatrician is amazed at this response, prompting the question, "How old is Donna now?"

"She just turned thirteen." The mom continues, "We all have chores to do each day in the house, everyone has to help out."

"Is Donna a good cook? Do you trust her to be home cooking dinner?" This is an unusual scenario in the upper middle class area. The mom responds, "She is a great cook, and she always cooks for us; it is one of her jobs around the house." The three other girls are attempting to chime in to tell their responsibilities. Seven-year-old Amanda announces with pride and a smile, "I have to clean the dishes after dinner." The nine-year-old Sasha announces, "I do the laundry!" The mom adds, "Even Aileen has a chore, she has to set the table each night." Aileen is the youngest and is twenty-eight months old.

The pediatrician turns to the three girls and asks, "Who is the boss?" The three of them answer, practically in unison and with big grins, "Mom and Dad!" The three girls are absolutely beaming with confidence, dignity, satisfaction, and sheer joy. They have boundaries and expectations and their parents are the boss! How wonderful for this family and the girls who clearly are thriving in an environment where they happily declare that Mom and Dad are the bosses.

If only more parents could follow their lead the world really would be a better place. It is very obvious that these young girls are growing up in a family where they are learning boundaries and how to follow rules. In turn, their road through school and into adulthood is going to be a much easier route. The work ethic that the mom is instilling now will last them through life. They are aware that Mom is the boss and if something goes wrong they have to answer for it. They are also aware that the smooth running of the household is, in part, due to their active participation. Their sense of self is being built up along with the humility involved in knowing who is boss and how to deal with being told what to do. They are also gaining the idea that teamwork pays off. The list of the good things they are learning goes on and on.

The meaning of being a boss includes your being in charge and the person who is the boundary setter. Take a running start with your baby because they grow so fast, and before you know it they will be adolescents testing your limits every day of the week.

Step 5

Become a Teacher

A teacher effects eternity.
He can never tell where his influence stops.

Henry Adams

A US historian, journalist, novelist, and educator,
the grandson of John Quincy Adams and great-grandson of John Adams

- You are your child's most important teacher

- Take the time to give your child explanations

- Find teachable moments throughout the day

- Learn with your child

This might seem like an obvious statement, but you may be surprised to learn that many parents don't understand their job as a parent includes being a teacher. This does not mean that the parent is standing in front of the whiteboard or the computer screen and doing physics problems, and this does not even mean teaching your child to learn letters. This is about teaching the most important skills of all—life skills. These include how to handle disappointment, figure out problems, deal with difficult people, and be a kind and caring person. These teachings happen each and every day in a parent's lifetime, and many are not even aware that they are happening.

This chapter is designed to give you a glimpse into understanding your parental role as teacher. Hopefully you will also enjoy being open to learning new things with your child, even if it means you have to look up the answer to a query like "Why does the sky look blue?"

Each parent faces a different challenge in order to fulfill their teaching role, since some children are less apt to learn than others. It is the combination of the skills of the parent and the learning style of the baby that will determine how easily success will come.

Let's start from the beginning. When babies are born, they are ruled by their brainstem; they are mainly reflexes. The theory of tabula rasa describes the newborn coming into the world as a complete blank slate only acquiring knowledge through experience. It is these experiences that shape the individual. There is no arguing that experiences have a profound impact on the type of adult he or she will become, but there is a much larger piece to this simplistic view of life—the old nature versus nurture theory is at work. Which one is correct? Does each baby grow up to be an adult that is purely the result of the sum of their life events as they are molded into the adult a parent wants? Or does the baby have a preset destiny determined long before birth as the DNA was intertwined into the baby's genetic code? The answer is no surprise as they both influence the development of an adult. The crux here is to put the nurture portion of the old argument to good use and potentially change the genetic destiny.

The cortex or thinking part of the brain has not fully developed at birth, but indeed it rapidly progresses, as a parent will obviously note their baby's first smile in response to a human face shortly after birth. That is their cortex doing the talking! The previously reflexive baby is now a thinking little being in a few short weeks. They are smiling at a human face! Going back to the tabula rasa theory that the newborn comes into the world as a blank slate and everything is a learned event, then the conclusion must be that the parent taught the baby to smile. Is smiling a learned response? No, it is not. Babies who are blind have never seen a smile yet they smile. Smiling is innate, programed into our DNA long ago. We can't and don't want to change that. However, it is not the smile that we teach the baby but the situations that will elicit the smile that a parent can help nourish.

The truth is every baby is born with a different set of genes and these genes program an individual to act in a certain manner. Take a tour in the newborn nursery to see the innate differences in the new babies within hours of birth. For example, Harry and Adam are two baby boys born within minutes of each other to a different set of parents. Both are in the nursery basinets while the nurses are busy working. Harry is in his basinet after feeding and is content to lie there taking in the new sounds, smells, and sights of the nursery. The time comes for Harry to be examined and he is undressed and poked and prodded by the pediatrician. Harry cries out during the more uncomfortable parts of the exam but quickly recovers and soothes himself back to his quiet state.

Now Adam needs to be examined. At first he is lying quietly in the basinet, but he quickly gets agitated at the interruption of his post-feeding bliss. He cries throughout the exam and is notably more easily startled than Harry was during his exam. Once the exam is over, Adam is still agitated and has more trouble calming down. He continues to cry. His *innate* self is hardwired a bit differently. He is having a more difficult time with his self-soothing mechanism than Harry did.

Now here is where things can start to go wrong. It is a natural instinct for all parents to want to soothe a crying baby. No one likes to hear a baby cry, so what do we do? We tend to immediately pick up the baby and do the work for him. We soothe him! It is only normal to react to a baby, but it's what we didn't do that is the more important piece here. The parent didn't attempt to teach Adam how to soothe himself.

Now stop thinking that he is too young and he is just a newborn. It is never too soon to start teaching your baby! All of his needs had already been met; he was fed, changed, clothed, and healthy. Letting a healthy baby cry for a short time, once all needs have been met, is good. You are starting to teach him how to self-soothe! You have to start somewhere, so start at the very beginning.

Adam can fuss and cry in his basinet and soon, chances are, he will calm down on his own. If Adam's parents respond to every gaggle or crying episode he has, he will not be given the chance to learn how to calm himself down. However, understand that common sense must always dictate, so if the sound of the baby's cry seems different or the baby is acting ill or not feeding well, seek out medical advice and respond appropriately.

Letting a baby start to learn how to self-soothe leads right into teaching a baby how to sleep. You don't actually have to teach a baby how to sleep, but you do have to teach a baby when to sleep and how to get to sleep and stay asleep, and teaching a baby how to self-soothe is the very first step. Teaching a baby good sleep habits is one of the most talked about topics in a pediatrician's office as the exhausted parents are begging for help. Start the sleep teaching from the day the baby is born and things will go easier, with the possibility of very long-term rewards.

Studies have shown that the baby's neuroendocrine system is affected by sleep. The neuroendocrine system has an effect on his future executive brain functioning that subsequently has long-term effects on the behavior of the child. Babies who have poor sleep habits at eighteen months may have a higher incidence of emotional reactivity, anxiousness, attention problems, and aggressive behavior as they get older. So teaching good sleep habits not only helps the exhausted parent; it has the more important benefit of improving the future brain function of the baby.

The newborn schedule is a tough challenge to most parents since babies' sleep-wake cycle is immature and longer sleep times don't usually occur till about eight weeks where we can expect a nice six to eight hours of sleep at a time. So the parent must start from the day the baby comes home from the hospital to teach the baby when to sleep and let them learn how to get to sleep.

When dealing with a healthy baby, each time you put the baby into the crib to sleep, make sure she is awake. Don't rock her to sleep. Don't let her use you as her sleep aid. No matter how good it feels to lovingly rock your baby to sleep, try hard not to do it. You can of course spend time rocking in the rocking chair and singing a lullaby and even reading books to your new baby, but don't rock your baby into a full sleep each night. If you do, this ensures that you have become your baby's sleep object and she will continually need you to help her fall asleep.

This means as she awakens throughout the night, you will again need to rock her to sleep, however long that takes, whether it's five minutes or even an hour. Your little baby won't care that it is 3:00 a.m. and you are completely and utterly exhausted. She wants and needs you to put her back to sleep since that is what you taught her. What needs to be done is you need to teach her how to self-soothe. This means she learns how to put herself to sleep and calms herself. You are being the teacher you need to be, you are not a bad parent! You are not abandoning her. You are teaching her essential self-survival skills that will only serve to help her!

The "abandoning" guilt that parents feel is of no use and is only harmful to your baby. Good parents are thinking about how their actions will affect the baby, they are not thinking about soothing their heightened emotions as parents, whether from guilt or worry or just the desire to be your baby's knight in shining armor. The parent who scoops up the baby and says, "It's okay, Mommy is here to make it better," is more likely appeasing their emotions than helping the baby. Who is the mom trying to make better? The baby is in a safe, beautiful, warm, cozy crib, well fed, has a clean diaper, and has parents that adore him. Sounds perfect, but the perfection is ruined if the parent continually gives in to useless guilt and misses out on the teaching opportunity at hand.

At some point when the parents get exhausted enough from the continual night awakenings, they start to realize that there is some sense in teaching the baby to remain asleep, and they have no reason to feel guilty or worried or feel like they are abandoning their baby. The sooner you start, the easier it is for everyone involved and every baby learns quickly!

A reminder to all parents to ensure good sleep habits, is that middle of the night feedings should be quiet with a quick diaper change, and then back to the crib. Keep the lights very low, as raising ambient light awakens the senses. Don't do any talking or singing, as this only reinforces the baby to wake up and feed. We want nighttime feeds to be short and without any stimulation. This teaches the baby that the middle of the night is for sleeping and not singing songs or having a mommy and daddy party.

This is just one example of how parents are their child's teacher. The list of how we teach our kids each day is endless. Again, this is not necessarily talking about how to make grandma's tomato sauce, although that is very useful as well, but more about learning important life skills. Teaching them not to bully other kids, how to be kind, polite, and treat others the way you want to be treated, and learning that when a parent makes a request it is followed—these are some of the more important skill sets that should be taught to our children.

Each child will present a different challenge in how well they absorb the parental teaching because, as discussed, every child is hardwired a bit differently. Some children are natural-born learners and people pleasers who make parenting easy, while others were meant to rock the boat a bit. The strong parent who keeps in mind that they are the teacher will continually reinforce the desired behaviors in the child.

Here is a common scenario where a parent may not even realize that teaching is happening but in a negative way. You are shopping with your toddler, Jon, in the lovely downtown mall when he realizes he would like an ice cream cone. He very sweetly asks if he may have an ice cream cone. His mom taught him how to ask for something and he even included the obligatory "please" in his query. His mom declines his request, gently reminding him that dinner is near and it is not time to eat ice cream.

What happens next? The typical experience with a toddler happens. Jon asks again but this time with a whimper and whine to his voice, "But I want ice cream!" The answer is again no. His mother is sticking to her resolve. So far everything is going well as his mom is not budging. However, sweet little Jon really wants this ice cream cone, and he is determined to get his way. Jon again asks but this time he is crying out loud, "I want ice cream! I said *please!*"

At this point people in the mall are turning to look at the little boy crying. The mom now starts to get a bit nervous and embarrassed and even angry. Her resolve is weakening, as she would just like her little Jon to stop crying. As she is pondering all this, Jon now throws himself on the floor into a full-blown tantrum. Most parents have suffered through this and can sympathize with the poor mother in the mall as they stare at the unfolding drama, feeling sorry for the poor mom but mostly happy it is not them dealing with this little toddler.

Jon is in a fever-pitch, screaming tantrum because he wants an ice cream cone, so his mom finally gives up and buys him the cone. After all, she wants to make him happy and stop his crying, but also feels the need to stop her embarrassment and provide some peace to the mall shoppers. As soon as Jon's mom announces that she will buy him an ice cream cone, the crying instantaneously stops. Jon is now happily eating his ice cream cone, his mom's blood pressure has returned to normal, and the mall shoppers continue with their day.

Unbeknown to Jon's mom, she has just taught him two very important lessons. Yes, indeed, she was absolutely teaching Jon some things. Lesson number one from this interaction is when mom says "no" it doesn't really mean no. It means maybe. Once a parent has said no it is very important to stick to that answer. Of course there are always exceptions but for the most part stick to your guns. If a parent is saying no at the outset and then changing their mind, the lesson the child learns is that no does not mean no. In the real world, no means no and it is important that Jon understands that as he grows into adulthood. The people Jon meets in the real world are not going to care that he is upset because he is not getting his way. His boss is not going to tell him he can't have a raise and then change his mind even if he asks seventeen times. Chances are this type of behavior will get him fired!

The next lesson she taught Jon is that crying and throwing a kicking, screaming tantrum will get him what he wants. So the next time mom says no, the very astute little toddler will cry and scream to get his way. That is a common learned response and one that should never ever be taught. Jon must understand that throwing a hissy fit will not get him what he wants as his life progresses. If his mom continues to teach him that tantrums and fits will be rewarded with his desires, it will more likely have very detrimental effects. Jon will grow up into an adult who feels entitled and demanding and who attempts to get his way by throwing "adult temper tantrums."

This may seem obvious when it is written down and it is being read in the comfort of the home, but when a parent is in the throes of dealing with a screaming, crying child, the only thing they want is for the situation to end. After all, who wants to hear their child cry? Who wants to see a child suffer the insult of not getting his way? Every parent instinctually wants to please their child and make them happy. Nothing is more gut-wrenching and viscerally agonizing than hearing your own child cry. It's perfectly normal to have all these feelings when dealing with a child who is hurt, disappointed, or crying because they did not receive something they wanted. The critical piece to this lesson is to remember that a parent's actions are forever teaching the child how to behave. If a parent succumbs to the child because they are having a crying fit, the parent is teaching them to cry and have a fit to get what they desire. We are teaching this behavior.

There are a few different ways Jon's mom could have handled this situation with a more positive lesson for him. Once Jon threw himself on the floor and started kicking and screaming, she could have quietly picked him up and left the mall, making sure that she did not start to raise her voice. The likely scene in the car would be that Jon would be crying the whole ride home and maybe continuing even after arriving home. His mother should not say a word to him as any attempt to talk with Jon or try to soothe him while he is hysterical ends up giving the child positive reinforcement for this negative behavior. If you attempt to soothe him during his hissy fit, you are teaching him that it is okay to act in this manner, and that is certainly not what we want to teach him. This is a very important lesson for a parent. Any time a child whines or cries, it is important not to respond to the child. You can give a gentle reminder, one time only, that they need to speak in a nice voice. Beyond that, it's better not to respond or give in to a whining child.

As soon as Jon has stopped crying and is quiet, his mother can now engage him. She should remind him that she is happy he was able to stop crying and when he is using his proper voice she can talk with him. By doing this she has taught him that crying won't get him what he wants and while he is crying he will not be able to talk with his mom to even attempt to get his way. This has also given him a chance to learn how to calm himself down, even if it meant taking him out of the mall. The next time he has a tantrum and he knows "no means no," the tantrum will be a little bit shorter. The following "no" may not even elicit anything more than a quick whine. As a parent teacher, the second scenario allowed Jon to learn much more useful life skills than the scenario where his mom gave him the ice cream cone in the middle of his tantrum.

Let us take a look at another example. A mom, dad, and their two children are eating dinner. The children are Tyne, who is thirteen, and Fabio, who is seven. The dad starts out with inquiring how the day went for his children. His son tells him that he had a great day since "we had a substitute teacher and didn't have to do any work today." His dad responds with, "Yeah, I loved those days in school, too. We used to torture the substitute teacher. I remember my friend Morty and I used to throw spitballs at the sub and we never got in trouble 'cause it was only the substitute teacher. It was hilarious! Ah, the good ol' days." Fabio loves listening to his dad's story as it validates his own experience at school.

Next up is Tyne, who did not have such a great day at school. She tells him that she is really upset and "hates going to school." Tyne's dad is perplexed since she is a good student, is involved in sports, and has lots of friends. "Why would you say that you hate going to school? What is going on?" Tyne proceeds to tell him about all the girls in school who have the newest version of the cell phone that just came out. "I am like the ONLY girl in my group who doesn't have the upgraded phone! That is *so* not fair. They all are like making fun of me. It sucks, dad, it just sucks!"

"I can't believe they are making fun of you for not having the upgraded phone, Tyne."

"Uh-huh, dad, they are. This phone is like a year old already. I asked mom and she said NO! I *need* to get the new one! I can't be the loser girl with the old phone!"

Her dad thinks about it for a minute and without conferring with his wife, who already said no, replies, "Well we can't have you being the only one in your group without the new phone."

"Okay, thanks dad, I knew you would come through for me."

Many parents can see themselves in this situation, as it is not an unusual one. What is important to see is where the teachable moments are and how they were used.

In the above scenario the dad essentially taught Fabio that it is perfectly fine to be rude to a teacher and not learn in class when a substitute is working. Regaling him with a story of his past days was fine, but he should have added that he felt really awful that he threw "spitballs" at a teacher and that he regretted his actions. As parents, life lessons are better given out to the children without a "lecturing tone"—using stories works.

As far as his daughter goes, the dad really screwed up here. In the first place, he completely undermined his wife and taught both his kids that their mother's decisions can be overruled and have no meaning. This happens all the time within families as one parent overrides another. It teaches kids that a marriage is not a partnership; instead one parent can overrule the other. No one wants that scene for a marriage!

The next learning point for Tyne was similar to the previous situation with the toddler and his tantrum. All Tyne had to do was whine a bit to her dad and she got her way. The dad gave in to her, for whatever reason, without even suggesting that if she wanted a new phone she should be the one to pay for it, or by telling her "Mom already said no" and ending the conversation. That would have been a better life lesson. Instead, she pulled a teenage tantrum and got her way.

The other point of Tyne's story is that she fell under the pressure from her "friends" to get a new phone or else suffer the insult of not having the newest, latest technology. She gave in to the "keeping up with the Joneses" idiom, which was reinforced by her dad. Again it is almost impossible to lecture a teenager and have it end up being an effective conversation that was taken to heart by the adolescent. You can talk to your teenager till you're blue in the face about "poor kids who have nothing, and look at what you have; why would you care if you don't have the newest phone? You have a new phone as it is, it's only a year old!"

The teachable moments happen all the time and through the teenage years the methods that parents use to teach their teenagers are more limited. The lecturing tone has to be kept to a minimum. Instead use past and present stories to help prove a point, even if you have to embellish them a little to make the lesson more enticing.

It is always important for the parent as the teacher to change *their* behavior for the better. It is so hard to be a parent and have to think about everything we do and say as parents. But we must continually remind ourselves that what we do and say will always have an effect on our most precious children.

Step 6

Teach Them How to Problem Solve

Creating something is all about problem solving.

Phillip Seymour Hoffman

From an interview by Tasha Robinson, Sep't 15, 2015, for the A.V. Club

- *Teach your children how to identify a problem*

- *Encourage them to find possible answers to a problem presented to them*

- *Ask them what each solution might look like*

- *Let them decide which solution they use*

What does problem solving really mean? It is a relatively new term, but the notion of problem solving has existed since the beginning of time when prehistoric man roamed the earth trying to figure out how the next meal would be attained. In the simplest sense, problem solving refers to figuring out one or many solutions to overcoming an obstacle. The obstacle can be a physical or nonphysical barrier that is blocking forward movement. How a person goes about problem solving depends on many factors. These include the type of problem presented, the capability of the person presented with the problem, their ability to identify that a problem even exists, their ability to formulate a plan, and then finally the competence of the individual to execute the solution.

Learning how to problem solve is an essential skill that is being lost in today's world. Parents are too quickly intervening in their child's life, Parents come to the rescue to solve school, social, or sports-related problems and are not giving their children the chance to learn on their own. The technology of the day is fueling the loss of problem solving by providing easily obtainable information and answers. Furthermore, parents are now merely a phone call away to solve any issue. With this generation losing the ability to solve problems, adulthood will be much more difficult to navigate.

Problem-solving difficulties can be manifested in many different ways. The emotionally labile child who throws a temper tantrum every time he is told he can't have a toy, or the adolescent who punches a hole in the wall at the slightest disruption of his day, has difficulties with *emotional* problem solving. The child who can't keep his schoolwork together, forgets books or assignments, refuses to do work around the house, or has trouble waiting his turn has more *functional* problem-solving difficulties. The child who has difficulty getting along with peers or uses bullying tactics has difficulty with *social* problem solving.

The child who does not learn to problem solve will start to avoid problems altogether. For example, if your teen is experiencing trouble in the locker room at school, he may deliberately cut gym class and avoid anything that has to do with sports. Instead of attempting to solve the problem, he withdraws. The child that is being picked on by a bully at school will cut class to avoid the bully. The child who becomes a bully to avoid group situations is lashing out because he may be unable to solve social problems. Many bad behaviors can circle back to a lack of problem-solving skills. Whatever the problem-solving challenge may be, it is up to the parent to help children learn the skills necessary to hone in on the abilities needed to be successful happy adults.

How children develop has always been affected by the technological advances of the day. The twenty-first century has the distinct advantage of having the computer age come to full swing, with most of the learning that occurs impacted in some way by computers. The ability to think is, however, not a technological advancement and will always be up to our human brain to control.

Critical thinking and problem solving go hand in hand. Critical thinking is the ability to synthesize, gather, and analyze information that was received from an event, from observation, from experience, or from reading. We are not fully sure how the advent of technology is affecting learning, but we are sure that it does have an effect. Whether obvious or subtle, good or bad, the new technology has an effect on the developing brain. The effects are not only obvious changes in the way children learn, but there appears to be an internal change as well. The neuronal wiring is affected by the new technology.

There is quite a bit of evidence that Internet addiction has very real effects on the brain. There is frontal lobe atrophy, which is the part of the brain that powers executive functioning or higher thinking. There also appears to be spotty loss of white matter and reduced cortical thickness, impacting higher thinking and functioning, emotional impulses, and cognitive tasks. Excessive screen time has proven effects on the developing brain, in particular the crucial frontal lobe, which guides every aspect of our lives, and it appears that the most profound effects occur in kids.

So the Internet does have effects on the brain, which we can extrapolate to affecting critical thinking and problem-solving skills. The actuality of this possible overall decline in aspects of the brain development may be sprinkled with the possibility that technology has the advantage of stimulating some aspects of learning in children. Some video games are designed to stimulate creativity, knowledge, reaction time, visual-spatial abilities, and problem-solving skills, and indeed they seem to do just that. The Internet also seems to be strengthening the ability to scan and process information at a much quicker pace. There are too many questions left to answer about the benefits or drawbacks of intensive computer use, but at the present time it is considered best to limit screen time, as many video games do not encourage development, but pull children into a mindless foray of violence and zombie killing that does nothing to stimulate thinking.

Reading helps develop critical thinking and problem-solving skills as compared to the visual learning of the Internet. The rapid pace of movement on the Internet causes one to skim over the information in a quick manner, never really assimilating all the information. Now with the added media aspect of the Internet, it appears that less stimulation occurs. Children learn better when presented with a document without distractions. Reading is stimulating to the brain, but less so when presented with videos and hyperlinks while reading on the Internet.

With the advent of the Internet, the potential to answer any question asked is at the fingertips of any child who can spell out a sentence—essentially most six- and seven-year-olds. The simplicity and ease with which a question can be answered presents some problems as well as advantages. The clear advantage is that information can be garnered quickly. Projects and homework assignments can be finished in no time, allowing for more fun time. If there is trouble learning how to do a math problem, the answer is sure to be found on the Internet.

The distinct disadvantage is that the information was attained too easily and quickly. Little to no thought was put into how to obtain the answer. It is quite possible that the answer could have been attained through a trial and error experiment or maybe through reading some articles and extracting the information after reading. Using critical reasoning and problem-solving skills are glossed over because the information is too easily obtained. It can be argued that if we don't use these skills, they will not stay sharp, or in the case of the growing child, the skills will never get a chance to fully develop.

Now add into the mix the overindulgent parent who rushes to help the child at the slightest hint of a problem. The parent who catches the child every time he sees the potential of a development of a problem and swoops in to fix it never gives the child the chance to develop the skills to solve a problem. There should not be a goal of prevention of all your children's problems. The goal should be to help them with the steps to solve problems when they inevitably occur.

Being able to properly engage in problem solving involves being able to first identify that a problem exists.

After the problem has been identified and defined, the next step is to formulate possible solutions. Using cognitive analysis and evaluating the resources available to solve the problem, the child can start to formulate the steps involved in solving the problem. After possible solutions have been thought out, the next step is to try the solutions to see if they work. It may take many attempts to solve the problem, but each failed attempt is a process in learning what didn't work and is another step toward sharpening the problem-solving skill set.

Let's take a look at how these skills develop from infancy to adulthood. Once we see how the development occurs, we will be better suited to help this generation strengthen their problem-solving skills.

When do problem-solving skills first take shape? We see babies in the first year of life start to develop these skills. Infants between six months and twelve months have evolving motor, perception, and cognitive skills that come together to start the problem-solving skill development. Infants are capable of understanding that biting a particular toy makes a squeaky sound. The sound may cause a reaction from the family dog, with the baby realizing a cause and effect. Now if the squeaky toy is not available, the baby is capable of banging another toy on the table to make a sound to elicit a reaction from the dog. Babies are smart enough to know that if a toy is sitting on a blanket, they can pull the blanket to bring it closer to them if they do not yet have the motor skills to crawl to get to the toy. This is problem-solving development in its literal and figurative infancy!

Parents can and should encourage these emerging skills by supplying toys that make sounds when touched or moved in certain ways. They should make sure the play environment has objects to grab the baby's attention, like colorful, textured toys. Encourage your baby's use of toys to get reactions from the environment. Use toys that require manipulation, like the pop-up box that opens once the proper place is touched, squeezed, or pulled. These reward-based games start to help babies "figure things out" and stimulate brain development.

The newest baby craze of using a DVD or flashcards to improve the baby's intelligence has no sound scientific basis. Studies have shown no difference in the intellectual capacity of babies who were exposed to educational flashcards and DVDs as compared to infants who were not exposed. It is more important for a stimulating, tactile, auditory, and loving environment to be the groundwork for fostering your infant's growth.

As babies move into the toddler years, problem-solving skills continue to develop. The toddler can now move around the environment and is able to start to manipulate the external surroundings. They can now see an object across the room and saunter on over to take a look. They can pick it up, throw it down, and put it in their mouth. So many new experiences are available to the very mobile toddler. Their hand dexterity has increased dramatically and they have figured out that they can put more food into their mouth by using a spoon. They are able to manipulate objects like blocks to build a tower. If there is a toy on top of a table, they are now capable of solving the problem of how to get it while it is so high up. They can push a chair close enough to climb and get the prize they are searching for. They are capable of more complicated problem solving. A marble stuck in a bottle may not be reachable with their little fingers, but they are quite able to figure out that if they turn the bottle over the marble comes flying out and is now in their possession. Again, more problem-solving skills have emerged.

Encouraging these problem-solving skills is a parental duty. By engaging your toddler to figure out simple solutions to issues, you are encouraging them to figure out problems. They feel wonderful when they figure out the marble comes out of the bottle by simply turning it over! Toys such as simple puzzles and shape sorters that encourage these skills are a good way to stimulate this development of problem solving. Have toddlers use push and pull toys as well as toys that they use their hands to create. Clay projects are wonderful for the young toddler to use their evolving skill set to mold and build. They can start to use their imagination and then plan out the steps to create a clay figure.

If your toddler comes to you crying that their toy is broken, try not to immediately rectify the situation. Let's say he comes to you crying that his favorite truck does not work anymore. He hands you the truck and on immediate inspection you realize one wheel has come off. Your instincts are to immediately go and find the wheel and put it back onto the truck. Instead, engage your toddler to show you what is wrong. If his verbal skills are good enough, he will be able to communicate that the wheel fell off. As the parent in this situation, an immediate smile and confirmation that he identified the problem correctly is in order. We want to try to always reward behaviors that we want to encourage. Now ask him how he thinks he can fix the truck. Get his brain to think about solving the problem on his own without his mom or dad fixing the situation.

It is never too early to start and nurture problem-solving skills. If his verbal skills are not advanced enough, it is still fine to ask how he thinks he can fix the problem. We are laying the groundwork for a critical-thinking problem solver to develop. He may point to the missing wheel or say, "Wheel gone." These words and actions should be met with a huge smile, "That's correct. Good that you thought about what was wrong with the toy." Little words of encouragement go a long way! You can continue the conversation by asking "How can we fix this?" If the verbal skills are good enough he may say, "Put it back on," or he may look at you in complete bewilderment. If no answer is forth coming, prompt him a bit. Ask him, "How can we get the truck to work again?" Let him think it over. You can prompt him by pointing to the missing wheel. He may not come up with the answer, but you are putting his mind into action to start to figure it out on his own.

Moving into the preschool years we continue to see the emerging problem solver. Children are much more social during this time and love to play games and interact with adults and other children. Their verbal communication skills have evolved and their command of language has emerged. Problem-solving skills can be nourished using their language-based skills. It is time to break out the board games. Any game that requires thought processes and planning ahead stimulates cognitive processes and brain connections that will help problem-solving skills develop. Simple games like memory card games and checkers are a good place to start.

While in the preschool years, parents should continually try to coax out thought processes in their child. This should be done in a systematic step-by-step way. This will help the parent organize their own thought processes while attaining the goal of stimulating the child to think through a problem and find his own acceptable solution.

Let's take the example of a four-year-old, Spencer, who is having a playdate with his friend Mike. Spencer decides that he wants the water gun that his friend is playing with, but Mike is not willing to give it up just yet. Spencer instinctually grabs it out of his friend's hand and accidently hits him with the plastic gun as he jerks it out of his hand. The friend immediately starts to cry, since he was just hit in the head, but more egregious in his mind is that his toy was taken away. Spencer is feeling upset that his friend is crying and the playdate has come to a halt.

At this time a parent can step in to try and help Spencer learn from this situation. First, try to have Spencer identify what the problem was in the first place. He may state that *he* wanted to play with the water gun. Encourage that answer, as it's the correct one. If Spencer is not forthcoming with an answer try to encourage him. Give him words to use like "It must make you mad to want to play with the water gun and have Mike say no."

Sometimes as parents we need to give words to the child. Angry, mad, frustrated, annoyed, and irritated are all words to help Spencer spell out his feelings at not getting to use the toy. Once the problem is identified, i.e., "I am mad because I wanted to play with the toy," the next step is to come up with potential solutions that don't end up in disaster. Ask Spencer what he wanted to do. He may reply, "I wanted to grab the toy and play with it so I did." Ask him if there are any other possible actions he could have taken. He may require coaxing, but let him do the solving. Prompt with questions like, "Do you take turns playing on the playground at school?" This may prompt a response from Spencer, "We could take turns squirting the water gun."

If he comes up with this solution, let him know "You thought of a good solution!" Praise the *process* of coming up with a resolution to the problem. He put some thought into the problem, which is the process a parent should praise. Reinforce thinking about other alternatives to an obstacle presented. It is also quite possible that Spencer may come up with an answer akin to, "We are not inviting Mike over anymore, I don't like him!" This should prompt the response, "Well what would you have done today if you didn't play with Mike?" These questions are designed to get Spencer thinking. Spencer may come up with, "I want to play with the toy and not Mike." Or maybe, "Let's put the water gun away and play something else." Whatever his answers are, it becomes an opening for more dialogue and brainstorming between the two of you.

The next step is to see how each solution will potentially end. Spencer's first response was to say he wanted the toy and took it. Ask him if the end result of Mike crying and the playdate coming to an end was really what Spencer wanted. His little mind will realize that it was probably not the best solution to his problem of wanting the water gun. Too much chaos ensued, and he could not enjoy squirting the gun. So then move on to the next response of the possibility of taking turns playing with the gun. This time hopefully Spencer will realize that if he had waited to take turns he probably would have been playing with the toy instead of having a conversation with his mom. The reward would have been much greater with this solution.

The other possibility of not inviting Mike over again is the last solution that you want to talk to Spencer about. Ask him what would have occurred if Mike didn't come over to play with him.

Maybe he would have been sitting in the den playing alone or watching television. Ask Spencer, "Would that have been a better solution for you?" You want Spencer to figure out the pathway or pathways that will end in the result that is most satisfactory to him. Now ask him which solution is best for him. Hopefully he will say, "I guess we could take turns using the water gun." The next step is to put the solution to work and test it out. If the solution is working well, reinforce the process that went into solving the problem; remind Spencer that it was good that he put the thought into solving his dilemma.

The positive reinforcement aspect is crucial, especially at this early age when they are still developing their sense of right and wrong. If the solution is not working well, the parent can step in and see if Spencer would like to try another solution that he came up with. Let's say Mike is really not going to let Spencer take a turn with his water gun. Now his mom can ask Spencer what *he* should do. Not what Mike's mom should do and not what Spencer's mom should do, but what *Spencer* should do. "Let's put the water gun away and play with the ball." "Okay Spencer, why don't you try that solution?" The point of this exercise is to keep the children thinking on their own instead of the parents rushing in to solve the problem, which is usually what happens just for the sake of simplicity and speed.

These daily events that happen in a child's life should be looked upon as ways to build up skills in the preschooler. Not every little blip will afford the opportunity to become a lesson in problem solving, as it can be time consuming, but it is good for the parent to understand how to take these scenarios that seem endlessly frustrating and build up the skills in your child.

These rudimentary steps to early problem solving that we should use to teach our preschooler are similar to a flowchart used to solve any obstacle. First identify the problem, then figure out potential paths to take around the obstacle, think about what the possible outcomes are with each solution, and then apply the solutions.

In the scenario above most parents will tend to run to intervene in the dispute between the two boys. Mike was crying, and it would only be natural for Mike's mom to console him and Spencer's mom to reprimand him for pulling the toy out of his hand. The next scene would be for Spencer's mom to demand he give an apology and make Spencer give the toy back to Mike. The opportunity for Spencer to figure out a better solution would not occur, since his mom already did it for him.

It is imperative that parents see these daily life scenarios as ways to help the kids do their own thinking and to stop doing it for them. Part of the everyday life of a preschooler involves problems, albeit little ones, that need solving. If a child has difficulty with problem solving and the parent is the one finding the solutions, the child will lose confidence and fall into a pattern of always needing help when an obstacle appears. This becomes a self-fulfilling prophecy of not being able to solve problems. The emerging perception will be one of someone who continually needs help with a problem.

As the school-age child grows, their ability to learn is dramatically increased. Their reading ability begins to expand exponentially, as does their memory. The school-age child can use logic, is able to see patterns, and realizes the meaning of cause and effect. All these skills are advancing and can be used to help sharpen their ability to problem solve. Now that they are older, more and more problems will arise. From fighting with siblings and friends to figuring out how to get their schoolwork done, their problem-solving abilities will be put to work every day. Parents must ensure that these skills are built up and not tamped down.

With the more advanced skills of the school-aged child comes more opportunity to facilitate creative and logical thinking, which are both skills needed for problem solving. Creative thinking allows one to see a problem in different ways and logical thinking breaks down the problem and analyzes each piece. Your role as a parent is to be an observer and supporter—as long as the child is safe—and see how they solve a problem. If needed, and only if needed, a parent can facilitate things.

Let's look at an example. Your daughter, Missy, has a best friend named Brittany who has asked her to help her cheat on a test tomorrow. If your child casually lets you know that, it is your job *not* to go into a tirade yelling at your child, "Are you crazy, do you realize how much trouble you are going to get into!" The last thing you want is your child to feel belittled and ashamed for letting you know private information in her life. The parent who starts off with negative comments will end up pushing the child away, and she will become more fearful of presenting an issue to you in the future. That is not the outcome wanted, but it is also not for you to give her the solution.

Here is where a parent will help their child build up the frontal cortex to figure out the answer. The parent can start off by asking open-ended questions to get Missy thinking. "What do you mean she wants you to help her cheat?" Remember, the first step to problem solving is identifying the problem. Make sure Missy is able to identify the exact problem. Cheating may not be a problem for her, but maybe the possibility of getting caught is the problem. She may come up with some creative thoughts. "Well, Brittany didn't bring her book home to study so she needs my help on the test tomorrow, but I don't want the teacher to get mad at me." Or maybe she says, "I am worried because how can I help her cheat since I am not sure if I even know the material well."

Observe your daughter as she thinks through this issue. What is the actual problem? Let her define it for you. You can facilitate some more thoughts by asking the question, "How do you feel about helping her cheat?" Let Missy think about that question. Her emotions may guide her to come up with a few solutions. Wait patiently, as you want to be a good listener and not jump in to say what is on your mind. Missy comes up with a few solutions, "Mom, how about we study together using my text book?" Or maybe she says, "Well, it's really not a big deal, I can let her cheat off of my paper tomorrow."

The second part to learning problem solving is coming up with solutions. The next part is seeing how the solution will work. The first response was an excellent solution to the problem presented to Missy. Ask her how the first solution she gave will work. How are Brittany and Missy going to get together? Let Missy navigate through the problem completely. Can they study using FaceTime? Does someone need to be around to drive back and forth? All the pieces to the solution that Missy came up with need to be put together to execute her solution.

Now let's go back to her second solution, which was to just let Brittany cheat off of her paper. Ask Missy what the possible outcomes of that are. "Well, chances are we won't get caught." As a parent we need to facilitate our child to learn a lesson, even if she gets into trouble. But ask her, "What if you get caught, how are you going to feel? Is it worth it?" Hopefully Missy will feel uncomfortable enough at the thought of getting into trouble that she will come up with an alternative solution. Stimulate her thought process, and let her be responsible for coming up with the path she is going to take. Make sure she thought through the possible consequences of her solution. All this is meant to have her work through the many paths. This is how to problem solve.

As the adolescent years come around, many more challenges are brought to the limelight. The Internet has evolved to serve as a second parent that has all the answers including, any guidance an adolescent thinks they could need. How to fix a broken lamp, how to paint a house, where to buy the best jeans, or how to pass the biology regents—all instantly answered just by typing in the question. With the possibility of any query being answered within seconds, it is so very important to make sure the groundwork for problem solving has been firmly laid down, as the temptation to shut down thinking is at the fingertips of every person.

The adolescent brain is not fully evolved and is run mostly by the amygdala, the area of the brain that controls instinct, fear, and aggression. Adolescents are more likely to, no surprise here, act without thought, get into fights, get into accidents, misinterpret social cues, and take risky chances. So now more than ever it is critical to stimulate your adolescent's problem-solving skills. The last thing we need is more people who lack the ability to see an obstacle and move around it.

Since the advent of the cell phone and the Internet, it is possible for teens to have their problems solved immediately with a phone call to a parent or by finding the answer from searching the net. Instead of the teen attempting to tough it out or figure out a solution without the use of a search engine, they are on the phone with a parent who has the problem taken care of before the teen finishes telling the parent what is wrong.

The teen may call his mom up because he forgot his lunch and has no money to buy lunch. The mom is there in a jiffy with his lunch. He lost the opportunity to figure out what to do without his mom coming to the rescue. He didn't have to starve. He could have decided to borrow money from a friend or even ask a friend to share some food just for today to get him through the day, but the immediate access to mom solved the problem.

The teen may have forgotten a textbook at home so he calls his dad to bring it up for him, immediately alleviating his dilemma. The cell phone has given teens the ability to have immediate contact with people who will rush to solve a problem for them instead of letting them figure it out for themselves, especially if it means discomfort for the teen. They are calling their parent for every little issue that arises since they don't have to have the challenge of solving a problem, knowing mom or dad are on the other end. This has left a big gaping hole in the problem-solving skills of teens. Let us fill this hole.

The simple framework of problem solving that children use still applies to teenagers, but can be expounded on, as the adolescent brain is capable of understanding and analyzing to a greater extent. The problem-solving cycle is what many psychologists refer to as the steps involved in problem solving for the more mature brain. Broken down, these steps are just a elongation of the steps younger children take.

The first step is always to "identify" the problem, meaning to recognize that there is one (For instance: My car is not working). The second is to define what or why there is a problem by looking at it from a different viewpoint or breaking it down into more detail (for instance: It must not be working because I left my lights on all night and now the battery is dead).

The next step is to organize the information needed to find out the different alternatives to solve the problem (For instance: I probably need jumper cables. But do I have any jumper cables? Do I need to call a mechanic? Should I just borrow the cables from someone if I don't have enough money to call a mechanic?), which leads to the next step of forming a plan, your strategy, to solve the issue (For instance: I will first ask the building super-intendent if he has jumper cables. If not, I will ask my friend to lend me money to pay for a mechanic). Then the plan needs to be implemented, such as by finding the money, objects, and people to help or the time needed to achieve the solution.

You then need to monitor the progress toward the solution, and the final step is to evaluate the end result. When teaching your adolescent how to problem solve, it is not always necessary to go through all the steps, as some problems are more easily solved then others, but it is important to make sure the adolescent has the framework to go through the steps when a more advanced challenge comes along. The parent needs to be there to be a teacher, observer, supporter, facilitator, and listener.

Let's take the example of an eleventh grader, Sally, who was suspended from the lacrosse team due to too many missed practices. She is an A student hoping to go to an Ivy League college and is very distraught over the suspension. The parent can sit down with Sally and facilitate a problem-solving strategy. Do not sit down and say, "What were you thinking?" Avoid accusatory terms like, "You should have . . . " or "Why didn't you . . .?" The point is to make this a helpful way to allow Sally to strategize.

First things first—what is the problem here? Have Sally identify the exact problem. Some eleventh graders may not find getting suspended from a few lacrosse games to be a problem, but Sally is clearly upset by this. She is relying on her lacrosse skills to get her into an Ivy League college and this suspension is devastating to her. Sally says, "The problem is I was suspended from the lacrosse team Ma!" The problem is easily identified.

Now you can help define or break it down into more detail. We know that being suspended from the team is the problem but much more defining needs to be done as the suspension is only the end result. Coaxing the use of creative and logical thoughts, ask Sally to put the problem into other words. "I am having trouble in my AP English class, so I have been staying after class for help which has interfered with my lacrosse practices." The problem is now being defined or broken down.

We have now identified the problem and defined it, by looking at it from different angles. Sally got suspended from lacrosse due to missing too many practices because of her academic trouble with AP English class. The parent's job here is to listen and be supportive and allow Sally to formulate more thoughts on the issue. "I missed a few homework assignments which made me fall behind in class and so I needed some extra help sessions." So now we are getting somewhere. We have identified that Sally missed lacrosse practices because she has been going to get extra help because she is falling behind in class due to missed homework assignments. By using creative and logical thinking, the problem has been identified and defined.

Some possible solutions now need to be sought. It is up to Sally to put together the next phase of identifying alternative plans to solve the problem, and then choose a plan. She then needs to implement her plan. The parent can ask, "What can be done next?" Avoid giving Sally the answers for a solution. We know what can be done, but it is the teen's job to come up with some possible answers. The temptation is to solve the problem and start to micromanage the issue. This is where most parents can't help themselves. They see their child in distress and immediately feel the need to resolve the issue for their child. This is not what a parent should do! Instead, await the response. Being a good listener and observer is a better strategy to help Sally. Do whatever you have to do as a parent to keep your mouth shut and just listen. The answers will come, and if you need to, you can do a little coaxing.

"I could stop missing homework assignments so I don't get behind in class." Solution number one is verbalized and it happens to be a solution that is easily attained. Positive reinforcement is in order, as you want Sally to feel empowered. Praise the process she is going through. She has come up with one solution and may come up with more, as she is feeling good about coming up with the first solution. Good emotions and positive feedback will foster the self-confidence needed to solve problems.

"I could get extra help in the morning before school starts so it doesn't interfere with lacrosse practice." Solution number two comes rolling off her tongue and is also a possibility. Now ask Sally if and how she can make them work. What is needed for her to get to school early? Will she need to rely on someone to take her to school? The logistical details need to be addressed. Once Sally has figured out how she can get to school early and is able to stop missing homework assignments, she will have solved her problem of missing lacrosse practice and avoid the possibility of future suspensions. The problem was solved by Sally. The parent did not jump in to save Sally, but was able to coax, listen, observe, and support to maximize this opportunity to let Sally's problem-solving skills get a workout.

What happens if a teen takes his car to school and comes out at the end of the day to find out the tire is flat? What is he to do now? It seems like a simple problem, but how to get it fixed is hard for the poorly-skilled teen. The first instinct is to call his dad. Teenagers are too adept at letting a parent solve the problem, and parents are too quick to solve it for them. If your teenager is old enough to drive a car, they are old enough to be able to take care of the car.

If they call you with this all too common problem, coax the solution out of them. "I understand the car has a flat tire, but how can I help you, when I am at work?" The teen response will be an annoyed, "I need you to get it fixed!" Parents need to stay in the positive and by giving the teen some reinforcement may propel him to continue on to figure out the steps to a solution. Staying calm is very important and now it is time to put the ball in the teenager's court. "How can you, yourself, fix it?" A typical response is going to be, "I can't fix it dad, I have never changed a tire in my life!" But the teen came up with one solution; he could fix the tire. Continue the dialogue and remember not to solve the problem for him. A teenager is perfectly capable of following the instruction manual that comes with all cars on how to fix a flat. The other option, if available, is to call a mechanic, but it is up to the teen to come up with that possibility and make the phone call.

Next, let us take a look at a more critical problem. What if your ninth grade daughter, Alice, comes home from school completely blindsiding you with an F in two classes? Clearly there have been problem-solving deficits that have gone unnoticed. You, as the parent, were unaware she was floundering in class and are not aware of any academic difficulties in the past. The micromanaging parent who never allows their child to fail will intervene by calling the teacher to demand an explanation and insist the grades get changed. This maneuver will not allow your child to deal with the consequences of failing, and they will miss out on a chance to learn a lesson in problem solving.

What would be an approach to make this a problem-solving lesson? First listen to what Alice has to say. Let her identify the problem in her own words. Encourage her to think about this issue from many different angles. "I failed math and science class!" is obvious, but we want more from her. The first step has been accomplished as the problem was easily identified. Sit and listen. Coax if you need to help her with defining the problem.

"Were you having trouble with the work all semester?" Avoid scolding her and asking why she didn't come to you for help. Let her figure it out. "Yes, Ma, I was having trouble." Encourage her to talk it out. Ask her open-ended questions so as not to sound accusatory. Have her write down the problem in her words and think about the issue from different angles so she can better define the problem.

She may suddenly realize that she was not paying attention in the classes because she was fighting with her best friend who was in the classes with her. Using creative thinking allows her to define the problem in different ways. She opens up and tells you the fighting with her best friend has been a terrible distraction in class, causing her to miss the crux of each lesson. The supportive parent will console her daughter and let her know that she understands. Thinking about the problem helped to identify that failing the classes was really a fallout resulting from the real problem. Alice's relationship with her best friend seems to be the crux of the issue.

Now Alice can be gently persuaded to supply some solutions. How can she make this better? She should be allowed to do all the thinking. Breaking down the problem and defining it helps to make it a much more manageable problem. She could reach out to her friend and attempt to work out their spat. She could attend all the extra help sessions and do some extra credit to make sure she passes next semester. What are the steps needed to get her extra help in class? Is this feasible for her? Let Alice do the talking! Do not intervene on her behalf! She will feel great knowing she solved her own problem.

Each day brings on little and big problems that need solving. How well a child can solve them depends on whether they learned to problem solve and how much they were able to exercise this skill. Parents must ensure that their progeny are fully equipped to enter the adult world having had every opportunity to learn how to be a creative and critical thinker, capable of identifying problems and finding solutions that can be executed with success.

If a parent is having a hard time following through on using life lessons to teach problem-solving skills, one only needs to be reminded that a child's brain is a muscle that needs to be flexed and worked to foster the proper connections for growth. This is scientifically proven. Using this scientific rationale, we can teach our children that just the act of thinking about a problem helps the brain connections grow. Children can have greater control over their destiny. They can actually have a say as to how smart they are or will become. This is a powerful tool parents need to use.

Step 7

Be a Good Example to Follow

Don't worry that children never listen to you;
worry that they are always watching you.

Robert Fulghum
Author of *All I Need to Know I Learned in Kindergarten*

- *Act the way you want your child to act*

- *They are watching you all the time*

- *They will emulate what you **do***

Do the things you want your child to do. It is extremely important to understand this step and take it to heart. Your child is forever watching everything you do and say. Your little girl yearns to be like you; she wants to wear mommy's clothing, put makeup on, and go to work like mommy. Your son wants to shave like daddy, play baseball and cook like daddy. The eyes of children are constantly on us, and we need to make sure we are "doing it right," as they will emulate much of what parents do, both good and bad.

Have you ever had the experience of saying or doing something and realizing that you sounded or acted just like your mom or dad? You may have used a phrase that your parent always used or maybe you reacted to a problem in the same manner as your parent did. Sometimes it's as simple as using a gesture your parent used. The feeling comes over you as soon as the words have spilled from your mouth, the reaction occurred, or you recognized your moms hand gestures while talking to friends. It's the moment you realize you have become similar to your parent. That good feeling or maybe not so good feeling of knowing that you have become your parent can take time to digest.

Sometimes it's an awful realization as you hear your mom's words come bellowing out of your mouth while yelling at your child. Words that you swore you would never use on your child. Or maybe it's the calm soothing way your mom spoke to you, never getting upset when you spilled a glass of water by accident. As a child, you were not aware that you were learning behaviors from your parents on a daily basis, but as an adult you realize the impact they had on your life.

Maybe you took away good habits or maybe you took away bad habits, but you definitely, unknowingly, took on some of your parent's behaviors. That is how important it is to make sure that as a parent now, you are setting the right example in everything you do! From cooking, to working, to exercising, to feeling good about yourself, to talking with friends and spending alone time with your family—everything is being watched and learned.

Since a huge part of parenting involves being a role model, you need to make sure you are practicing what you preach. Children are being imprinted with parental behavior from the minute they are born. They want to be mom or dad. Now that you have a new baby it's time to take on the habits that you want to instill in the baby and maybe get rid of some bad habits!

One merely has to listen to the Harry Chapin song "The Cat's in the Cradle" to understand how important setting an example is. The premise of the song is about a young dad trying to raise his family while working hard to pay the bills. He is away on business when his son learns to walk and misses this milestone. Then when the dad buys him a new ball he is too busy to play with him. The little boy continually promises to his dad that he wants to grow up just like him, as every little boy does. However the dad is spending his child's formative years working and feeling exhausted, leaving no quality time to spend with his little boy.

The dad is completely unaware of his shortcomings as a father because he is too busy trying to be a provider.

Now as the boy grows into a man the father finally has time for his son and would like to spend time with him. But when the father asks to spend some time with his son after he arrives home from college, the son would rather borrow the car keys than sit and talk with his dad. The example he set while his boy was growing up was that of a hardworking father who never made time for his family. Now the son is grown with a wife and kids and his dad calls him up to ask to spend time with him, but it's too late. His son turned into him! He's a hardworking man who never learned how to make time to spend with his family.

It is too late for the dad to reverse the example he set for his son while he was young because his son is a grown man now. It is very emotional to think that your child may grow into an adult that may not make time to spend with you. All it takes to prevent this is to ensure that you spend quality time with your child. This means planning each day to have a least some time where your child knows that it's his time with his parent. This must occur continually throughout his childhood. The emphasis is on quality, not quantity.

Studies have shown that parents who stay at home tend to spend less time interacting on a quality level with their children than working parents. The typical day of a stay-at-home parent involves many tasks and chores, and although the child is with the parent most of the day, it is not true quality time.

It's easy to see how a day with a stay-at-home parent leaves them with the feeling that the whole day was spent attending to the needs and wants of the child. The natural assumption is that the child had an immense amount of attention from, and quality time with, the parent. However, looking closely at the day, it becomes apparent that not much time was actually spent interacting in a stimulating, positive way.

Let's take a closer look. At the start of the day, mom or dad is busy making breakfast while the child is watching the morning TV shows. (Television use in the early years should be severely limited.) The mom or dad then needs to tend to household chores, including washing clothes, cleaning floors, paying bills, yard work, and so forth. Next up may be a shopping trip for food, clothes, or other household items. Once shopping is done, there may be some free time to meet with a friend and have a playdate. The moms are interacting while the kids are playing. The visit comes to an end and it's time to cook dinner. The television goes on again. The working parent comes home and the rest of the evening is spent cleaning up after dinner and preparing to get the child into bed.

The day may seem filled with child and parent time, but it is the quality time that takes precedence. A parent can spend the whole day with a child and never realize that all they did was give the child commands, tell them what was going to happen in the day, or maybe even continually reprimand him.

The mom and dad need to make sure that quality time is being spent with their child. This means no distractions, no phone calls, no television, and no other people in the room taking your attention away from your child. This is one-on-one time. That is what children thrive on! This quality time does not have to go for hours. It can be done in short, bite-sized periods but your only focus should be on interacting with your child. This can mean coloring or throwing a ball around or playing dress up. Whatever the activity is, it is meant to spend time talking and getting to know the little human you brought into the world. Ask them about what they like and how their day was, or what they did at school or who they played with, or what the teacher said to them. It is these quality times that will make a difference in your child's life.

The parent who works all day and comes home to spend the last hour of the day focusing totally on their baby usually spends more quality time than the parent who is home all day with the child. Remember, it is the context of the time spent, not the amount of time spent. Ideally the working parent should set aside time at the end of each day to be with each child individually. This allows each child to talk about their day without the competition of the other children.

By spending important time with your children, you are setting the example that family matters. It also gives you the opportunity to better know what is happening in your child's life, even if it's only your two-year-old's account of gymnastics class. This is the message you want to send to your kids no matter how old they are. If you are the parent who was always too busy to sit and read a book or play ball with your child, she will grow up having learned the same skill set.

So lead by example. If you tell your child to eat his vegetables, then you better make sure that you are eating those vegetables as well. You can never expect your child to do something that you are not willing to do. When I give advice to parents on eating well, I have to first make sure the parent will partake in healthy eating. How can a parent prepare a vegetable filled meal and expect the child to eat it if the parent doesn't?

It's a situational oxymoron. As an adult, if you don't eat vegetables, and you don't value the inherent disease-preventive value to ingesting them, but are trying to teach your child to eat them, you are setting yourself up for a very difficult task. This may actually serve to help parents become healthier eaters, and there is no better motivator then your children. If eating your fruits and vegetables gives your children a better chance at eating healthy foods, then why not do it?

Exercising on a regular basis is another good place to start. You can take your baby for walks or jogs. Even going to the gym with the baby or being with the babysitter at the gym is a good way to start to teach your baby to exercise. This may seem too young to you, but nothing is too young when it comes to teaching your child good habits. They are absorbing everything around them all the time. One of the fundamental health habits is exercise!

Getting good amounts of physical activity is a crucial part to getting and staying healthy. Parents must instill this habit in kids, but it is impossible if they do not participate. Imagine telling your child to go outside and get some exercise while you are in front of the TV or computer. Why should your child go out and run around while you are inside vegetating.

Doing fun family exercise activities together is a good way to instill the habit in your child. From bike rides to long walks and park play to swimming, all are part of being a good example to your kids. Doing these kinds of activities as a family is not only good for everyone physically, but it has the added benefit of being a stimulating bonding experience as well.

How about the amount of television or computer time? Limiting that useless downtime and being more creative as a parent will help your child develop better.

Your children will grow to be very much like the example you set whether you like it or not. Even if you are trying to teach them not to be like you, chances are they still will end up similar to you.

Step 8

Don't Give Them Everything They Want

Your children will not remember you for the material things you provided, but for the feeling that you cherished them.

Richard L. Evans

Richard L. Evans' Quote Book

- *Stop the material overindulgences*

- *Spoiled children are self-centered, greedy, and place less value on human relationships*

- *Spoiled children strive less to achieve*

It's hard to imagine that parents who opt to continually satisfy their child's "heart's desires" are more likely harming them than helping them. Every parent craves the sensation they feel when they see their child happy and smiling, and it is even more wonderful when it is the parent that put the smile there. Their intent may be good, but does overindulging your child really satisfy them? Is it a good idea to say yes to most things your child asks for?

No parent wants to see a child feel sad, and when everyone is walking around with the newest, coolest backpack, they want their child to be included. The thought of your adolescent being the only one not driving a new car once she passed her driver's test is unbearable, so you absolutely must get her a brand-new car lest she feel left out! Your daughter wants the new $150 jeans everyone is wearing and it is impossible to say no since "everyone has them but me, Ma!" Your kindergartner is shopping with you and with his big, blue eyes and a big smile asks, "Daddy, please can I get this cool car. It's my favorite. I am saying *please*," and it is impossible to say no and turn his little smile upside down.

The list is endless, but at some point the buying frenzy has turned many kids of the current generation into spoiled, materialistic children who can't understand what it means to be grateful and appreciative. The research is clear on the end result of parental overindulgence and it's time to slow down the spending and let the kids work a lot harder to achieve material items.

The words "spoiled brat" is a derogatory term and implies being flawed or having "gone bad" as a result of getting every whim satisfied. In the United States, parents of infants and toddlers spend 3.3 billion dollars per year on toys and over 40 percent of world revenue on toys is spent in the United States despite having less than 4 percent of the world's population of kids.

An even more unnerving statistic was the rise in toy sales at the height of the recession despite the housing market, stock market, and pretty much every other industry hurling downwards. It seems American parents feel the irresistible urge to give their kids as much as they possibly can and, even if they can't afford the toys, somehow their kid will get them. The nation today is more affluent than it was seventy years ago and parents naturally want to indulge their offspring, but as is the recurring theme in this book the pendulum has swung a bit too far and this generation is turning out to be the "I can get whatever I want" generation.

When a new baby is born, no one wants to shower this precious new life with toys and clothes more than the parents. They worry about which toys are best to stimulate the baby and help her develop so they pay an extraordinary amount of money for the squeeze toys that will "enhance your baby's senses." They fill the toy box with toys even before the baby has arrived and the toys keep coming in droves after the baby is born. Before you know it, the baby's room is filled with so many toys it is impossible to keep track of them all, as they are buried in piles of toys in the closet, toy box, and toy shelves. Because there are so many toys, it is quite possible that a good number of the toys never even get used. According to one estimate, more than three billion dollars of the toys consumers bought go unused.

It may be a surprise to parents to find out that having all these toys is not helpful to your growing baby, despite what the toy industry is saying. Take the scenario of three-year-old Sola at her birthday party. She is sitting in the middle of a pile of twenty or so presents that have been showered upon her. Her excitement is tangible and she starts to open up her presents. The first one is a set of dolls, which she is ecstatic over. She starts to play with them but gets distracted by the opening of the next toy, which is a toddler laptop computer with word games and puzzles. Her excitement intensifies as the next toy is opened, and the next and the next.

One after the other they are opened and set aside. She also received some new, beautiful outfits, which are opened and thrown on the floor as they are of little interest to Sola who already has a closet full of new clothes. At this time Sola is sitting amongst a dozen or so toys and she doesn't know which toy to play with since there are so many to choose from. Instead she gets up and starts to play with all the paper on the floor from the wrappings.

This is a common scene that many parents can relate to. The child has so many options that it is causing too much stimulation and distraction, and Sola is unable to focus on any one item. Toy overload is happening and this is not good for the child. It is hard for any parent to imagine that receiving just one or two toys is more than enough for their child, but studies are pointing more in that direction. This does not include books, as they are always stimulating to the mind and can be the focus of an interactive time with the parent. Even before a child can read, it is not unusual to see children leafing through the pages of a book and making up a story as they go along that enhances their imagination and creative play.

However, when young children have too many toys, they actually spend less time playing than children who have just a few toys. When there are fewer toys, it forces the child to learn to play. Their imagination can run wild when there is just a ball to play with or some leftover cardboard boxes. They can build forts and hideouts and interact with each other instead of having fifteen toys to choose from, none of which require much imagination. They also tend to have more solitary play as opposed to interactive play when there is a plethora of toys available.

Parents will also spend less time interacting one-on-one with their child when options are bountiful. So cutting back on the number of toys our young children receive is a wonderful idea. As one mother of four girls said, "I let them have their birthday party and then I let them pick out two toys. The rest I take back to the store and get money which I put into their college fund." This may be a hard sell, but her children are better off for it.

One reason for the overindulged child seems to be due to parental exhaustion. Parents are working out of the home to provide for the family and come home too tired to say no. It is much easier to say "Yeah, sure you can have the new truck" and see your kid smiling and happy, which means he is quiet and content. Or you can say "No, you can't have that new truck now, but maybe for your birthday" and then have to hear the whining and see the sad face.

The other factor that may be driving the spoiled child syndrome is parental guilt for having to work outside the home. Many parents feel guilty that they are working and have to spend so much time out of the house and away from their child so they attempt to compensate the child by giving them everything they ask for. They strive to make every moment they spend with their child as pleasant as possible, and saying yes makes them happy! But the end result is a child who expects to get every material thing he asks for. This gets his brain used to seeing something and getting it, which is not what we want for our kids.

Let's look at George, a nine-year-old boy who has lovely parents who are lawyers that work outside the home. They both spend long hours at work and have the typical feelings of parental guilt because they can't be home every day when George gets home from school. George is actually quite lucky, as he gets to see his grandma each day, since she is there for a few hours until his mom gets home from work. Once his mom gets home, all attention is on George and his needs. He has a room filled with every gizmo and gadget a kid his age could want. His mom makes sure that George never feels disappointment since "he must feel it every day when he comes home from school and I am not there to get him off the bus." Despite what his mom thinks, George is having a wonderful life, thanks to his hardworking, tired, guilt-ridden parents.

Peeking at a day in George's life, we can see where the direction of his life is going. George wants to go to the amusement park with his friend and George's grandpa is more than happy to oblige him. Since George is an overindulged only child, he is insisting on being the first one on each ride. His grandpa gently reminds him to take turns, but George is not listening. He is oblivious to the fact that his friend is waiting his turn while George gets to go first each time. When playing arcade games George wants to take some tickets from his friend, who begrudgingly gives him some, so he can get the biggest prize. While they are sitting at lunch George accidently knocks over his friends soda and does not apologize nor does he take responsibility for the accident and claims, "I didn't do it, it's not my fault!"

As the afternoon is winding down and it is time to go home, George decides he wants to get an ice cream cone. His grandpa, who has witnessed his grandson's behavior all day, finally says no because it is "too close to dinner and we are going home now to eat the dinner that Grandma cooked." George starts to whine saying, "But grandpa I *really* want an ice cream cone." The whining escalates into a full-blown, crying tantrum because George is not used to being told no. George's friend, a little boy himself, who did not particularly enjoy being with him at the amusement park, is now flabbergasted at seeing his friend throw a temper tantrum like a little toddler would. This is not the way a nine-year-old acts!

Unfortunately for George, he is acting like a spoiled child typically does. He is like the child Veruca Salt from novelist Roald Dahl's *Willy Wonka and the Chocolate Factory.* "I want it and I want it now!" He is demanding to have his way and it is not his fault because no one taught him the word "no." George is displaying behavior typical of a spoiled child. He lacks consideration for others, is self–centered and greedy, refuses to take responsibility for his actions, and throws tantrums that he is too old to be displaying.

None of these characteristics are good ones, and most parents would prefer not to have children with even one of these traits. A child like George is in a loving home with a grandmother who is there for him each day. There is no reason for his parents to feel guilty and cave to his every whim and spoil a child who could be well adjusted and "good." The fallout is so much worse than getting used to saying no to George.

George and Veruca Salt are extreme examples of spoiled children, but most parents can relate to being too tired and having feelings of guilt propelling them to say yes more times than no. The point is to start to recognize how destructive we are being as parents when we succumb to the whims of our children because of our own feelings.

Taking small steps to being less indulgent will go a long way. Start by making your child earn a reward. If they want to get the latest toy fad that everyone has, insist they spend their own money. If they don't have any money in their piggy bank, then let them start to earn money by committing to daily chores in the house. Starting off small is a good way. For instance, if your seven-year-old daughter wants to get a new accessory for her bike, let her pay for it with her allowance. This allowance should only be given out weekly once her chore of emptying the dishwasher each night is completed. If your twelve-year-old son broke his snowboard and needs a new one, but the holidays are over and his birthday is months away, he should pay for it.

Children who get everything without paying for it tend to be careless and ungrateful. They don't value what they have, since a parent can easily replace it. The child who has to work and save money to purchase an item will be much more likely to take good care of their hard-earned prize.

Overindulged children who value money and attention are less likely to value relationships and less likely to contribute to society. This bears repeating: They are less likely to value relationships, which is what life is all about. They view material objects as more important to their happiness than having a valuable relationship with another human being. Teens who view themselves as spoiled also tend to have lower grades, are more likely to cheat on tests and cut school, and are not as content as their peers. The spoiled teen does not place a high value on academic achievement. It is understandable not to feel the need to achieve academically if everything is handed to you, since most people go to school so they can get a good job that fulfills them and hopefully make money to buy items they enjoy. If it is handed to you, why bother to work for it?

There is absolutely nothing wrong with working hard to attain a material item, even if it is frivolous. If it is your hard work that is making the money to buy it, then you are entitled to do whatever you please with the money. As parents, however, we have a greater responsibility to do what is right by our children and that means to stop indulging them no matter how good it makes you feel.

Driving past the local high school, the parking lot is filled with brand-new cars like BMWs, Mercedes, and Porches. New drivers not even of legal age are driving cars that most people strive their whole life to save for. What is the point of giving a young child a brand-new, high-end luxury car? What have they done to achieve such a material reward? Who are we helping by giving everything to them so easily at this tender age? The teenager who has not worked to attain something of worth cannot comprehend its value.

Studies have shown that adolescents who described themselves as being spoiled are also more likely to have behavior problems. Nothing good comes from giving a child everything they want when they haven't worked for it.

The spoiled child syndrome is epitomized by a story told by the mother of a son who was killed in an auto accident. She lectures high school students as part of driver's education classes in high school. No alcohol or drugs were involved in the death of her son, just a fast car. The mother tells the story of how her beautiful son was killed when he was a passenger in a new sports car that was driven at excessive speeds by his friend.

Her story is meant to bring reality to the new, young, would-be drivers who are about to grace the roads. It is meant as a warning of how dangerous the roads are and how not only drugs and alcohol, but high speeds can kill. She describes the horror of how her son died at the hands of an irresponsible adolescent who was driving a sports car, given to him by his parents, that he was clearly not able to handle. He should have never had access to the sports car.

She continues the story by telling the audience how the parents of the son driving the car purchased another brand-new sports car for their son after he had not only crashed one car but killed her son at the same time. "What kind of parent indulges their child to such an extent?"

The gross emotional injury to the mother whose son was killed is evident as she relives the story she tells to high school adolescents. This demonstrates the extremes of an overindulgent parent, and while we don't know where the young man who was driving the car is now, it is a solid bet that he is not a successful man. He was given too much too soon with the most awful result, and even with that he was quickly rewarded with a new replacement sports vehicle. His parents essentially set him up for failure for the rest of his life, not taking into account that he has to live with the knowledge that his reckless driving cost the life of his friend.

Parents must put aside their own feelings and think about how much it benefits their child when saying no. It is hard to change habits, and the tired, guilt-ridden parent is the perfect target for the manipulative child. It is crucial to let them learn how to work for something instead of giving it to them when they want it. We don't want a world full of children like Veruca Salt; remember what happened to her?

Step 9

Don't Be Their Friend

If you want to be treated like a mother, act like one.

Jeannette Walls

Half-Broke Horse

- *Being bosom buddies with your children results in them not respecting your leadership*

- *Being close friends with a parent becomes a burden for the child*

- *Don't treat a child like your bosom buddy*

Many parents may see this step as a not very important one. The new generation of parents feel that there is no real harm in being a friend to a child and may even see it as a necessity to encourage a good familial bond. Unfortunately this is far from the truth. The parent that treats their children like a friend runs the risk of raising angry, depressed, and neglected children. Yes, neglected children! The data is very clear and there should never be a time when a parent puts their child in the friendship role. Children need to be treated like children. Treating a child like a friend puts them in a position they are not ready to handle. They are too young to handle adult issues, whether they are fun issues or serious issues, they should never be put in a position to act as a friend to their parent.

Imagine this scenario. Carla, an eleven-year-old girl, is having a sleepover with her best friend Lola. They want to go out to see a movie and they are looking through the possible choices. Carla picks a PG-13 movie but Lola turns to her and says, "We can't see that movie, we are too young; what are you thinking?" Carla responds in disbelief and says, "Wow, it's not such a big deal, when did you get so old?" They pick out another movie that is more acceptable for their age group and off they go.

At the movie theater, Carla is messily eating popcorn and it is spilling on the floor. Lola reprimands her and says, "Oh my god, Carla, stop being a slob and spilling the popcorn on the floor. Someone has to clean up after you, be a little more considerate." Carla rolls her eyes and ignores the comment. They finish the movie, go home, and go straight to bed. The next morning they wake up and have breakfast and are planning the rest of the day together. Lola reminds Carla, "You have to clean your room before we can go out, so get to it." Carla, having had enough, replies, "Since when did you become my mother? I will let you know if I need another mom so stop telling me what to do!"

The role that Lola is taking on is costing a friendship. Lola has been treating her friend as if she were the caretaker of Carla. As is the case with real friendships, Carla is not going to stand for the demands Lola is making. No one wants a friend barking out commands and acting as a moral compass and she is certainly not going to listen to a friend reprimand her. She is not her mother, after all. She is a friend. Looking at this situation, it is easy to see that when a parent takes on the role of being more of a friend to a child their role as parent becomes diminished. The child views the parent as being on the same playing field and therefore will not respect the parent when the time comes. It will become much more difficult for the child to follow the consequences the parent has doled out because friends don't give out punishments to their friends.

The definition of a friend is someone we have affection for, we enjoy being with, someone who makes us feel good when we are with them, has mutual likes, supports us when we need them, listens to our problems, accepts the not so good side, and gives advice when we ask for it.

The definition of a parent is someone who nurtures, teaches, coaches, sets limits, morally guides, and provides food, shelter, and love to a child. Some of the particulars of friendship and parenthood may overlap a bit, but by no means is one comparable to the other. For instance, it is acceptable for a friend to lend an ear to listen to problems, but it is expected that a parent listen to their child's problems and then offer advice and guidance. It is not the job of a friend to give reprimands for stepping out of bounds; it is the parent who is expected to dole out the consequence.

The lines of friendship and parenthood are pretty easily delineated and the "jobs" should remain separate. Parents may be under the notion that being a friend to their child will ensure that their child likes them. This is propelling many parents to blur these lines, trying to be the cool dad who hangs out with his kid smoking marijuana while he is telling him about his "asshole of a boss." The mom who hangs out with her fifteen-year-old commiserating on how "creepy" all her daughters high school teachers are is not doing her own job but the job of her daughter's friends. The parent is under the mistaken belief that this type of behavior, being a friend to her child, will nail the good parent award and provide the groundwork as a good role model. Unfortunately parents who blur the lines of parenthood and friendship with their children are attempting to assuage their own needs while universally harming the future of their own child.

This does not mean you shouldn't have fun with your kid. You absolutely should get on your hands and knees and pretend to be the horse giving rides, playing ball, going on roller coaster rides, watching movies together, and playing games. Spending time with your family is what gives life meaning and we all should do it with gusto, however the way you spend time with your adult friends is very different from the way time is spent with children.

A parent should not give the impression that their child is their peer or "equal." It is imperative that the parent asserts their role as the boss since children thrive on rules and boundaries.

Listening to your young child talk about his experiences and spell out the details of his day is a parental job. Letting your children have their voice heard and letting them express themselves is a key part of development—it gives children a sense that you care, which is important for their self-esteem and security. Being approachable is a valuable tool in the parenting toolbox. This means your child should always feel the door is open and you are safe to talk with. This does not mean letting your child interrupt a conversation or use inappropriate language nor does it mean he can tell you whatever he wants without the possibility of redirection or even a consequence.

Take Harry for example, a normal, rambunctious eight-year-old boy who comes home from school and tells his dad, "I punched Paul in the nose today. We were on the bus and he bumped into me, so I punched him. He is a jerk anyway and I don't like him. The bus driver didn't see so I didn't get in trouble." His dad replies, "Did you use a left hook or an uppercut? Ha! Just kidding with you son." His dad leaves it at that and no more is spoken of the situation. Maybe his dad was proud that his son could throw a punch, maybe he was glad his son was not the one who got hit in the nose, or maybe he felt empowered by his son acting like a "man."

Whatever the case, his father responded as a friend would have in this situation. Rather than inquiring about Harry's disdain for this young boy and counseling him on how to behave, he joked about the situation. He let a perfectly good teaching opportunity fall into the gutter. His father needed to delve into this story in a calm manner and not end it with a simple joke.

Children will meet other children they don't like throughout their journey in their early years, and parents should be there to guide them. There are times we don't like somebody "just because," but most of the time there is something in the person that reminds us of what we don't like about ourselves. Harry's dad could have asked his son to try and think about why he does not like Paul. Let Harry's brain grow a bit while he tries to give a reason. He may not know and chances are he may shrug his shoulders and say "I don't know" or he may say "Dad, he is just a mean kid. He picks on the younger kids on the bus."

Whatever reason Harry gives, it's his reason. His dad can then expound on it by helping Harry figure out ways to handle the situation a bit better next time. Telling Harry, "You will meet all sorts of people in your life and you can't punch each one of them in the nose just because they bumped into you," is a start. The next steps to this scenario should have Harry walk away with a lesson on how he could have handled this situation a bit better. His dad could take him on a problem-solving journey: Define the problem, give possible solutions (that don't involve punching in the nose), and execute the possibilities. Because Harry's dad was trying to be the "cool parent" he lost the opportunity to learn from this experience.

Michael is a thirteen-year-old boy who has always been a good student and had a lot of friends. Recently he has been starting to act out in school. He was sent to detention two times in a week for using foul language directed at his math teacher. The principle suggested he talk with the school psychologist about why he has been behaving badly in school. The school psychologist has been evaluating Michael and has diagnosed him with depression. He suggests Michael come to regular therapy sessions, which he is compliant with.

Once the therapist starts to have a rapport with Michael he notes that he is extremely casual and not respectful of his title, always calling him by his first name despite being asked not to. The psychologist also notes that Michael uses a plethora of slang and foul language throughout the conversation, not minding how offensive some of the words may seem to an adult.

The psychologist starts to get a sense as to what may be going on so he starts asking more direct questions about how Michael's parents interact with him. Michael tells the psychologist, "My parents are the greatest. My dad is like my best friend. He is really cool." The psychologist continues to ask more specific questions. "What do you mean your dad is your best friend? Don't you have friends in school?" He responds with, "Yeah, of course. But my dad, he is really my bud. He never yells at me and he lets me express myself, he doesn't get on my case about shit and lets me be. He is just, ya know, a cool dad. All my friends wish they had a dad like mine." The psychologist has figured out the problem.

Michael is not thriving in an environment where his parents are his "friends." He craves discipline, guidelines, and boundaries despite not overtly realizing it. He is feeling alone because he lacks leadership. The years of having his parents act like friends have left him feeling depressed, and he's acting out as a result. When the parent is the leader in the household, the children will follow with respect. They learn how to respect other adults and feel safe and secure. If the parent continually acts as a friend to the child, it becomes difficult for the child to understand not only how to interact with adults but children in this situation feel like they are walking on a circular path with no direction.

They feel all adults are their friends and act in such a manner. If parents set the precedence that their child's friends can address them by their first names, it becomes a given that he will feel perfectly fine addressing other adults by their first name without being invited to do so. If the parent allows foul language directed at adults and does not correct the behavior or even encourages it by cursing and cajoling back, there is no surprise when he is behaving the same way in school amongst his teachers. It is what he has learned. It is not his fault. Treating children like a friend only hurts them in the long run. Letting your children know that he or she is not your peer and making sure the proper boundaries are followed helps avoid these misdirected actions.

Some parents may not even be aware that they are acting more as a friend than a parent. The easy adolescent who does well in school and helps around the house without being asked may have needed very little boundary setting in the past, making life easy for the parents. These parents may tend to "slack off" and act more as a friend to the child.

If you are the parent who has been on the path of a close friendship with your child, it is not too late to change direction. Making small changes can have big effects. When your child comes home from school complaining that, "The stupid dress code in school doesn't let me wear midriff tee shirts," instead of agreeing that the dress code is stupid, remind her that there is always a reason for dress codes even if it is not always obvious. Her friends are there to agree with her and trash the school dress code, but the parent needs to stay in the proper role and make sure the child abides by the school's code.

The adolescent who gets caught texting in school and gets his phone taken away by the teacher will likely come home saying, "Mr. B is such an asshole. That jerk took away my phone for the whole class. I wasn't even texting, I took it out to look at the time. Really, Ma. He is a tool and I swear if he does that shit to me again I am gonna rail on him." The parent who is the friend will sympathize with him and encourage him: "Yea I don't blame you. That sucks to get your phone taken away, I would have been pissed off too." It is understandably annoying to have a cell phone taken away, but the parent must be the parent and not the friendly sympathizer. A more appropriate response is, "Well if Mr. B is teaching class, it is rude to take out your phone, and next time it won't happen because you will keep your phone in your backpack where it belongs during class. Anyway, you need to be paying attention to the teacher and not the phone." This will of course illicit some eye-rolling and moaning and groaning but that means you did your job as a parent.

When kids are with friends it is expected that they act a bit silly and mischievous. When they are with their parents they can also be silly, and the parent can be goofy with them without stepping out of the parental role, but once the mischievousness occurs, the parents need to put the brakes on. The parent who is at a celebratory bat mitzvah with his thirteen-year-old son on the dance floor spinning around like a top (possibly much to the chagrin of his son) and singing songs with all of the kids is having fun with his son and enjoying the party as it should be.

However, when the boys all go over to the bar and start throwing back vodka shots, not only should the dad not be there with them drinking, he needs to put a stop to it. The parent may get caught up in the moment and let good sense fly away by taking a shot with the kids and thinking, "Everyone is having a ball and what harm is a shot or two of vodka anyway?" The dad gets the momentary thrill of having all the kids think he is great because he participated in underage drinking, but ultimately he is acting as a poor role model and will not arouse respect in the long run. Taking the role of a friend leads your own child into feeling disoriented. It is okay to be the fuddy-duddy. That is what parents are supposed to do, and kids expect it and feel safe when parents are acting in their defined role.

Being silly with your kids is a great way to bond with them and let them know that you still have some inner child alive inside. Letting loose with the kids is very different than being their friend. For example, if you take your son's baseball team out for lunch after a game and in the car the boys are telling dumb jokes and making farting noises with their armpit, it is fun to have a dad laugh along with them and even give them pointers on how to make the perfect farting noise with a wet armpit.

But if while waiting to be seated in the restaurant your son takes a napkin and wipes off all the specials that were written in chalk on a board in the front of the restaurant, it is not okay to laugh. He is being mischievous. His friends are there to laugh with him and his father is there to tell him, "That was wrong, and someone now has extra work to rewrite what you just erased. Now go tell the manager what you just did." While driving in the car the dad was being silly along with the kids, but as soon as his son was mischievous he stepped into the parental role and addressed the issue.

Divorced families or families where there is marital discord are particularly vulnerable to wanting to turn a child into a friend. One parent may be more emotionally fragile and feel the need to draw closer to the child. The mother or father may be worried about being the "bad" parent now that there is not a united front and will allow the child to do things that were not allowed in the past.

Let's see what this might look like. Dylan is a nine-year-old boy who spends half the week with his mom and the other half with his dad. He is a typical kid who likes baseball, hockey, and video games. When Dylan is at his dad's house, he spends time worrying about his mom being alone, but his dad assures him that she is fine and there is nothing to worry about.

His dad has very strict rules and makes sure Dylan follows them. He has to have his homework done before dinner, he gets thirty minutes of video game time, and bedtime is at 8:00 p.m. sharp. Dylan complies with the rules, and his dad treats him just as he did before the divorce saying, "Rules are rules and these are mine and you have to stick with them." He never talks about Dylan's mom unless it directly involves a situation with Dylan.

The scenario is different when he's with his mom. She often talks to Dylan about her problems. "I hope I have enough money to pay the rent this month." Dylan replies, "Mom, you can have my money, and maybe I can get a job and do something. I am the man of the house and I should help out." Dylan is already concerned about his mom when he is not there, and now he is more worried about making sure the rent is paid.

His mom also discusses his father: "I had a fight with your dad today. He was such a jerk when we were married and he is an even bigger jerk now. I don't know how I ever married that man." She asks Dylan's opinion about adult issues, "Do you think I should switch banks? Other banks are offering better rates. What do you think Dylan?" He gives his opinion, not really knowing what it means. When she comes home from work she recaps her day with Dylan, leaving few details out, including telling him about the "gorgeous guy who hit on me today. Oh that felt good to have someone notice your hot mom!"

If his mom is asked to go out for an evening she talks with Dylan first to make sure he is okay with it. When it comes to doing homework, he is allowed to finish it whenever he wants and is even allowed to play video games before his schoolwork.

His mom put a television in his bedroom after his dad moved out, so now Dylan can watch it late into the night without a set bedtime. Because his mother is anxious about losing her son's love, she does not want to enforce the rules and is talking to him like a friend. She is even relying on him emotionally as a shoulder to lean on.

Dylan is acting more like the parent in this situation. His mother is, in a sense, emotionally neglecting him by treating him more as a friend and confidant than as a child. His emotional needs are second to his mother's needs as she is acting more like a needy friend than his mother. This type of behavior, if not identified and altered, will have long-term negative effects on Dylan.

This "emotional parentification" is a term coined by psychologists to describe the role reversal when children are put into the position of taking on the role of providing emotional support to the parent. This happens too often when a troubled parent at a time of crisis turns to the child for support as one would turn to a friend in a time of need.

There are many levels of emotional parentification, from being a parent who is a bit immature and worrying too much about wanting their kid to like them, to the parent who turns to their child as a confidant in all aspects. Sometimes a parent might not even be aware they are looking to their child for support. They feel they are being appropriate and acting as a "hip" parent. Other times the parent is so desperate and lonely that they are relying on their child to listen to their problems and give them advice. Single parent families and families with marital discord are more likely to have children who are emotionally parentified; however, it can occur in any family.

There is a spectrum extending from emotional parentification, which is at one extreme, to the parent wanting to be the friendly hipster parent at the other end. The concept here is that the roles of adult and child are blurred. The outcome of this situation is universally harmful to the child as they grow to adulthood. The child ends up feeling emotionally neglected and angry. They have more trouble communicating with adults and difficulty with spousal relationships. Placing a child in the role of an emotionally supportive friend puts a tremendous burden on their little psyches. They always want to please a parent but are not prepared to take on the responsibility of being a friend to a parent. They are not equipped to deal with the personal details in their parent's life—it is beyond their scope of abilities.

Even adolescents who feel they are mature and can handle anything have difficulty with the burden of a parent acting more as a buddy than a parent. They rightfully don't want to make decisions with their parent that does not directly involve them. The parents are also barking up the wrong tree if they think they will get some good advice. Adolescents are inherently self-centered and think mainly about what is going to affect them and their social life. When a parent comes to an adolescent looking for guidance on how to search for a new job, or how to handle a difficult boss, or where to invest their money, they are asking them questions that are far better directed to a peer. The adolescent cannot and should not handle the burden of being asked advice on adult situations.

The parents that have put the child in the friend role should recognize this is inappropriate and change their behaviors. A parent that feels the need to include a child in all their activities is too involved on a friendship level. This can easily be stopped. Don't ask your child for permission to go out; it is not up to them and they don't need to know about every move you make.

Don't lean on them emotionally, no matter how tempting. Don't ask their advice on adult issues. Don't share your worries with them; they don't need to handle your worries. They will have a lifetime to worry over their own issues. Don't try to impress them by acting in juvenile ways that are outside normal parental boundaries.

Be empathetic to their plight when they are the ones who have difficulties, but as the adult in charge, make sure they are sticking to the rules and being respectful to authority figures like teachers, other parents, and police officers.

Being a parent means we must take on many roles, but the role of being your child's friend should not be one of them.

Step 10

Don't Try to Make a Doctor Out of a Novelist

*Nothing has a stronger influence psychologically
on their environment, and especially on their children,
than the unlived lives of the parents.*

Carl Gustav Jung

Psychology and Alchemy, Collected Works of C. G. Jung

- *Your child is not a smaller version of you*

- *Don't try to fulfill **your** desires through your child's life*

- *If you plan every step of your child's future, it becomes your life, not theirs*

After years of therapy, Elliot, a medical student from Indiana, has finally come closer to figuring out why he has anger management problems. Ever since Elliot was born his mother promised herself that her new baby boy was going to receive the best education and become a doctor, so she spent the better part of Elliot's young life telling him that is what he was going to do.

During the years that Elliot was in grade school his day was planned from dawn till dusk by his mom. Elliot had tutors to help ensure that he performed at peak level. Even Saturday playdates would be cut short so he could attend his tutoring sessions. As his mom arrived to pick him up, Elliot would plead, "But Mom, please let me stay? It's Saturday and there isn't any school and I did all my homework." His pleas fell on deaf ears. "Elliot, how do you expect to be a doctor if you don't go the extra mile?"

Every now and then the parent of a playdate would be taken aback when hearing his mom mention becoming a doctor. "Gina, does Elliot want to go to medical school? Isn't he a bit young to know what he wants to do?" Her response was, "I always wanted to go to college and go into medicine, but my life got sidetracked. I don't want that to happen to Elliot. It's very important to me."

So Elliot's mom persisted in carrying through with her plans for him, drilling it into Elliot's head that he would be a great doctor. But if you asked Elliot what he wanted to be when he was in third grade, he would say, "I would like to be a judge on the Supreme Court, or maybe a baseball player. I am really good at baseball, so, yeah, a baseball player would be cool. But my mom said I am going to be a doctor so I guess I am gonna be a doctor. I am very smart you know."

Once Elliot entered middle school his personality started to change. He started to become quiet around his parents and developed a sad aura that went unnoticed by his consumed mom. He was outgoing and fun to be with when his friends were around, but he started to develop a bit of a temper when interacting with his parents. The early teen years are usually a tad difficult, and it did not seem that Elliot was any different from his friends, who were attempting to defy authority and find their own way.

The difference was that this teenager, who had been told every step of the way that he was going to be a doctor, was not sure that medicine would be right for him. He loved to write, and although he knew that he was better suited for writing, he would not allow himself to pursue this since his "destiny," as foretold by his mom a million times, was to be a doctor.

Throughout high school he started to act out and became occasionally quite defiant. In Elliot's developing mind, he felt like he could never talk with his parents about his issues. He felt his needs didn't really matter to his parents; he felt that all that mattered to his parents was what they wanted. He eventually stopped looking to them for guidance since his voice was never heard. Instead he turned to his friends for advice on important matters that should have involved his parents.

Elliot continued to live with the burden of knowing in his heart that he did not want to be a doctor. He felt as if he had no choice in the matter, since it had been so ingrained in him since he was a young boy. Not even realizing why, he became an extremely resentful and angry teenager, and at one point he even started to become withdrawn from his friends. All the while he continued on the path that was set before him.

The story of Elliot is not an unusual one. Parents frequently push their children into careers, and some may not even be aware they are doing it. Many family businesses continue on because the children are groomed to run them. Of course there are plenty of people who have benefited from inheriting family businesses, but it should never be at the expense of individual happiness. Elliot experienced many of the problems that occur with children whose parents insist on a career path. His mother saw Elliot as a part of herself, which made it easier for her to transfer her unfulfilled ambitions to him. He was the surrogate for her dreams. This occurs more with parents who see their child as a part of themselves rather than as a fully separate person.

Elliot became embittered and withdrawn. His desires were not important and he started to act the way he felt—invisible. He unknowingly withdrew from his parents, not seeking advice from them and limiting communication. His internal anger churned because he felt like a helpless captive on a ship taking a course he did not want to take.

Unfortunately for Elliot, he is currently an angry, resentful medical student who did as his parents wanted but to what avail? The path that his mother set him on was not his path but was instead his mother's dream.

The theory of "symbolic self-completion" is when a symbol, i.e., a child, sports star, or movie star takes on the role of an unfulfilled desire in an individual. A father who dreamed of being a professional musician may become a groupie of a famous band and live his dream through his identification with the band members. A mother who went on to try to be a ballet dancer but had to give it up because she became pregnant now follows and cheers for the career of a professional ballet dancer. This gives her a sense of completion as she identifies with the dancer that she wanted to become.

The safe and harmless symbols that people use to help attain a feeling of wholeness for unfulfilled dreams include famous athletes, actors, and musicians. Being attached to them is an innocuous way in which people can attempt to find resolution to the incomplete fulfillment of their dreams. They feel and see the world through the eyes of their symbol and feel successful along with them as long as the outside world is also watching the success of the well-known person.

However, when a parent uses their child as a symbol for self-completion they become less worried about their child's internal happiness and instead are more concerned about other people observing their child's success.

Guiding and counseling a child is different from pushing and forcing them into something. Having expectations is not the same as planning the route for your kid. For example, you may be the mom who almost made it to the spelling bee championship who now has a daughter who seems to be a good speller. You can guide her and ask her if being a competitive speller is something she would be interested in, but demanding she compete is unfair to her. If you continually push her to spell competitively and she comes in last every competition or is just not interested in being a champion speller, you might be suffocating her ability to have any fun in other rivalries for now or in the future. When a parent forces a child into participation they may lose interest in the activity.

Parents are generally not good judges of their child's talent. They are so blinded by their love for their kids that it is impossible for them to be an objective evaluator. Unfortunately, this can cause them to push a child into continually failing. As discussed, having failure is not always a bad thing since we need to learn how to handle and recover the lack of success, but being forced to perpetually fail at a task that a parent is pushing a child to do is a completely different matter. It is better to listen to teachers and coaches when it comes to assessing the skills of your child. This applies to sports as well as academics and careers.

Don't confuse having expectations for your child and making sure they have outside activities with pushing them into a specific career or sport. Children who have lots of activities tend to do better than those who do not. In the past, the "over scheduled" child was thought to have more stress and anxiety but this is not the case. Kids who are kept busy do better on many levels. They are less prone to participate in negative social behaviors and are healthier and better adjusted.

However, your child should always be given the option of which activity they want to participate in. There is nothing wrong with insisting that a child do a physical activity and a non-physical activity each semester, but let them choose from a set of possibilities. If your child abhors team sports they can be offered options of gym class, karate, or dance, and so forth. There is no reason to force a child to do a particular sport, but there is every reason to have the expectation that they engage in some sort of organized physical activity.

As they pick out what they want to do, you are there to guide them. The child must be the one managing his or her path and desires. Offering a child a piece of paper with a pencil to draw something on is different from giving them that same piece of paper and pencil and telling them to write a sheet of music.

If you see yourself planning your child's future career, stop dead in your tracks. You are setting them up to become resentful and potentially really miserable adults.

If a parent maps out the steps of their child's life, it is then indeed not their life they are living; it is the parent's life. All parents need to do is counsel them, give them guidelines, cheer them on, and occasionally redirect them, but let them steer the ship.

Conclusion

I know that being a parent is the most important and the most difficult job on the planet, which means we must continually strive to do it to the best of our abilities. It becomes very important to be able to objectively observe your actions with your children and recognize if things are not going well. The ten steps takes the complicated task of parenting and breaks it down so you can see each aspect clearly. It is my hope that parents now and in the future will raise a generation of "almost perfect" children.

About the Author

Photography by Matthew Starr

Mary Ellen Renna, MD, FAAP, started her career after graduating from New York University School of Medicine in 1986. She is board certified in pediatrics and also carries a certification as a Physician Nutrition Specialist. She has spent her career in private practice and has devoted her life to the well-being of children.

She is regularly called upon to appear on television as a medical expert on various pediatric topics. Appearances include *The Today Show*, *Fox & Friends*, WPIX's morning show, *Good Day New York,* and *Long Island Talks*.

Dr. Renna has published two books, *Growing Up Healthy the Next Generation Way* and *Medical Truths Revealed*. She has authored many articles on pediatric medicine and was a regular contributor to *Woodbury Magazine*.

Her active interest in combating the obesity epidemic led her to become a spokesperson for Apple & Eve's health program for children, with her face appearing on millions of juice bottles. Currently Dr. Renna works with several brands marketed for children, including Earth's Best, that strives to offer healthy options for children as they grow. She is also the spokesperson for RX Safes, a company that manufactures devices used to help minimize drug abuse from prescription medications.

She has received multiple awards for her work as a pediatrician, including an award from the foundation Autism Speaks, the Cooley Anemia Foundation Humanitarian of the Year, the Multiple Sclerosis Foundation Humanitarian of the Year, Compassionate Doctor Award, AAP Education Award, and the Stony Brook Education Award. She was recognized as a leading professional in the Long Island Top 50 Most Influential Women in Business.

Dr. Renna is an active Fellow of the American Academy of Pediatrics. She has three grown children and continues her private practice in Jericho, New York.